Steve Kowit seems willing
to take almost everything into his arms.

—Ron Koertge, poet and novelist

Steve Kowit:

This Unspeakably Marvelous Life

With Illustrations by Mary Kowit

Edited by:
Duff Brenna
Walter Cummins
Clare MacQueen
R. A. Rycraft

Adapted from the *Serving House Journal*
"Steve Kowit Memorial Edition"
(Issue 12, Spring 2015)

Steve Kowit: This Unspeakably Marvelous Life
With Illustrations by Mary Kowit

Edited by:
Duff Brenna, Walter Cummins, Clare MacQueen, and R. A. Rycraft

ISBN: 978-0-9862146-6-0

First Serving House Books edition: 2015
Published by Serving House Books, LLC
Copenhagen, Denmark and Florham Park, New Jersey, USA
www.servinghousebooks.com

Front-cover concept by Duff Brenna; cover design by Clare MacQueen and R. A. Rycraft; book design and formatting by Clare MacQueen and Walter Cummins.

Photographs of Steve Kowit are the sole property of Mary Kowit, and are reproduced here by her permission. Illustrations are copyrighted by Mary Kowit and reproduced here by her permission.

Please send questions and comments to Duff Brenna at:
servinghousejournal@gmail.com

Dedicated to Steve and Mary Kowit

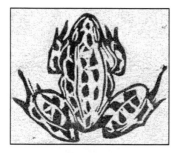

Table of Contents

Contents, Continued

Contents, Continued

Contents, Continued

Contents, Continued

Credo

I am among those who believe
different things on different days

—from *Lurid Confessions*, by Steve Kowit

Brief Bio
(June 30, 1938–April 2, 2015)

At *Serving House Journal* (SHJ), we are heartbroken by the loss of our dear friend and colleague, the acclaimed poet, editor, and teacher Steve Kowit, who passed away at his home in Potrero, California on the second of April. He was seventy-six.

Steve joined SHJ as our esteemed Poetry Editor in 2010. He published hundreds of wonderful poetic works in our journal—to be specific, 371 poems by 152 poets in Issues Two thru Twelve.

He described himself as "a poet, essayist, teacher, workshop facilitator, and all-around no good troublemaker." A founding member of the San Diego chapter of the Jewish Voice for Peace, he lived with his wife Mary and several companion animals.

Steve taught poetry workshops in San Diego, and his handbook for writing poetry, *In the Palm of Your Hand: The Poet's Portable Workshop*, is widely used. His most recent collections include *The Gods of Rapture* (City Works Press, 2006), *The First Noble Truth* (University of Tampa Press, 2007), and *Lurid Confessions* (Serving House Books, 2010).

His final collection, *Cherish: New and Selected Poems,* is forthcoming soon from the University of Tampa Press.

"A strong and vibrant force for poetry," and a true mensch, Steve will be profoundly missed.

Introduction

As Steve liked to say, he was Jewish by birth, Buddhist by inclination. We like to think he will be remembered as a *bodhisattva mensch:* an enlightened and extraordinary man whose mission seemed to be to help others become better at their art than they thought they could be.

Steve Kowit was a man of integrity who wrote and spoke Truth, often in a very direct way. He was a generous, ebullient spirit who helped folks for the sheer satisfaction of helping; an unsurpassed teacher who used hilarity to edify and instruct his students; and a jocular personality overflowing with love and laughter—yet feisty enough to point out the foibles of humanity on a regular basis. He was an authentic human being who genuinely cared; an outspoken champion of human and animal rights; and a kind-hearted soul who was mindful of all sentient creatures down to the tiniest insects that most of us never notice. His eyes were wide open to the miracle of life and how precious and fleeting it all is.

In other words, he was someone to emulate—whenever and wherever possible.

Perigee lauded Kowit when his third full-length collection of poems, *The First Noble Truth,* won the Tampa Review Poetry Prize in 2006: "His spirit, intelligence, and humanity never cease to amaze us. Not to mention his particular talent for poetry which is both profound and accessible."

Novelist Duff Brenna calls Kowit "a major figure in poetry in America today" and "the best lecturer and commentator on the craft of creative writing that I've ever seen in action."

Steve Kowit (pronounced "COW-it") was born in New York City in 1938. He was educated at Brooklyn College in New York (B.A.), San Francisco State University in California (M.A., 1968), and at Warren Wilson College in North Carolina (MFA in writing, 1992). He taught

English and creative writing for 46 years, including two decades at Southwestern College in Chula Vista, California; and he regularly toured with his popular poetry workshops.

Numerous awards have been conferred on Kowit, including among others the National Endowment for the Arts Fellowship in Poetry, two Pushcart Prizes, the Atlanta Review Paumanok Poetry Prize, the Oroborus Book Award, the San Diego Book Award, the Tampa Review Poetry Prize (as mentioned above), the San Diego Book Award, and the Theodor S. Geisel Award in 2007 for *The Gods of Rapture.*

With much gratitude and love for Steve, we offer this memorial edition of *Serving House Journal* (online and in print) to commemorate his life, which was dedicated to Poetry, to his beloved wife Mary, to his students, to humanity, and to the circle of all sentient beings who suffer.

—Clare MacQueen,
Associate Editor and Webmaster
Serving House Journal

In Memory of Steve Kowit:

http://www.servinghousejournal.com/KowitMemorial.aspx

A Few Words about Steve Kowit

Kowit's 2006 collection of poetry entitled *The Gods of Rapture: Poems in the Erotic Mood* was praised by U.S. Poet Laureate Billy Collins as "poetry that marvelously inhabits the adjoining rooms of the past and the present."

Montana's Poet Laureate Sandra Alcosser said, "*The Gods of Rapture* could provide an erotic daybook of the year. Pace yourself and prepare to be seduced."

Kowit's work appeared regularly in magazines and journals and has been read by Garrison Keillor on National Public Radio. Kowit was the recipient of a National Endowment Fellowship in Poetry, and the winner of two Pushcart Prizes. His latest collection of poetry, *The First Noble Truth,* won the Tampa Review Prize for Best Collection of Poetry for 2007. Charles Webb, author of *The Graduate* and numerous other works, said: "*The First Noble Truth* is a green oasis where the water tastes sweet and makes me laugh, makes me feel warm and comforted, glad to be alive."

Webb's quote is apt. If you read Kowit, you too will feel warm and comforted. You will feel glad to be alive. And we might add: you will feel intellectually engaged and enlightened and you'll want to go online and buy all of his books, and you won't be sorry if you do. Kowit was one of the great poets of his generation, and we were very fortunate to have such a huge talent as a member of our editorial staff.

—Duff Brenna
Founding Editor
Serving House Journal

Books and Chapbooks

Steve Kowit produced five full-length collections of poetry, with the newest, *Cherish,* forthcoming soon from the University of Tampa Press.

His guide to writing and appreciating poetry, *In the Palm of Your Hand: The Poet's Portable Workshop,* is used as a teaching manual in workshops, colleges, and universities across the country. He also edited *The Maverick Poets* and translated into English Pablo Neruda's final book, *Incitement to Nixonicide and Praise for the Chilean Revolution.*

Kowit's books and chapbooks are listed on the next two pages by date of publication, in reverse chronological order.

Full-Length Books

Cherish: New & Selected Poems
(University of Tampa Press, 2015)

Lurid Confessions
(Serving House Books, 2010)

Crossing Borders,
with art by Lenny Silverberg
(Spuyten Duyvil, 2009)

The First Noble Truth
(University of Tampa Press, 2007)

The Gods of Rapture
(City Works Press, 2006)

In the Palm of Your Hand: The Poet's Portable Workshop
(Tilbury House Publishers, 2003)

The Dumbbell Nebula
(Roundhouse Press, 2000)

The Maverick Poets
(Gorilla Press, 1988)

Incitement to Nixonicide and Praise for the Chilean Revolution,
by Pablo Neruda and translated by Steve Kowit
(Quixote Press, 1979)

Chapbooks

Intifada
(Caernarvon Press, 2005)

Steve Kowit Greatest Hits 1978-2003
(Pudding House Publications, 2004)

Epic Journeys, Unbelievable Escapes
(State Street Press Chapbooks, 1998)

Pranks,
with illustrations by Lenny Silverberg
(Bloody Twin Press, 1998)

For My Birthday
(Caernarvon Press, 1997)

Everything Is Okay,
with drawings by M. Jeanne Willoughby
(Gorilla Comix, Gorilla Press, San Diego, 1985)

Passionate Journey: Poems & Drawings in the Erotic Mood,
with Arthur Okamura
(City Miner Books, 1984)

Cutting Our Losses,
with drawings by Louis Griffith
(Contact/Two Publications, 1982)

Hearts in Utter Confusion: Takes on the Erotic Poetry of India
(Dog Ear Press, 1982)

Selected Blurbs

Crossing Borders

Tough, poignant. . .drawings and poems addressing the international epidemic of refugees. . . .

[He's] the most raging, socially concerned, funniest dead serious poet I've ever met.

> —Robbie Conal, author of the introduction and one of the
> country's foremost satirical street-poster artists

In the Palm of Your Hand: The Poet's Portable Workshop

An illuminating and invaluable guide for beginners wary of modern poetry, as well as for more advanced students who want to sharpen their craft and write poems that expand their technical skills, excite their imaginations, and engage their deepest memories and concerns. Ideal for teachers who have been searching for a way to inspire students with a love for writing—and reading—contemporary poetry, this book is used in high schools, colleges, universities, and writing workshops across the country.

> —Tilbury House Publishers

The Dumbbell Nebula

Whether describing the Devil reciting poetry in Hell, the fate of uprooted mice, or a last encounter with a doomed friend, Steve Kowit's poetry has chosen, in the manner of Sufi tales, a disarmingly earthy presence. Rhapsodic and hilarious by turns, the poetry is as engaging and accessible as vivid prose.

—The Roundhouse Press (from the book's back cover)

The First Noble Truth

Steve Kowit's poetry is shamelessly accessible, written in something close to the real language that we speak. Yet in Kowit's hands it is language that is both luminous and lyrical. His poems are sometimes hilariously funny, sometimes fiercely political, sometimes slyly anecdotal, and sometimes all these things at once. His latest book, winner of the Tampa Review Prize for Poetry, will confirm the observation of Thomas Lux that Kowit "has more energy, more passion, more fire, and more humor in his left little finger than most poets have in their whole bodies."

—The University of Tampa Press

The Gods of Rapture: Poems in the erotic mood

[. . .] praised by U.S. Poet Laureate Billy Collins as "poetry that marvelously inhabits the adjoining rooms of the past and the present." Montana's Poet Laureate Sandra Alcosser said, "*The Gods of Rapture* could provide an erotic daybook of the year. Pace yourself and prepare to be seduced."

—from "A Few Words about Steve Kowit," by Duff Brenna

[From *The Gods of Rapture*]

What chord did she pluck in my soul
that girl with the golden necklace
& ivory breasts
whose body ignited the river:
she who rose like the moon
from her bathing &
brushed back the ebony hair
that fell to her waist
& walked off
into the twilight dark—
O my soul,
what chord did she pluck
that I am still trembling?

    after Chandidās

First Portfolio:
Selected Poems by Steve Kowit

Poetry, in the end, is a spiritual endeavor. Though there is plenty of room to be playful and silly, there is much less room to be false, self-righteous, or small-minded. To write poetry is to perform an act of homage and celebration—even if one's poems are full of rage, lamentation, and despair. To write poetry of a higher order demands that we excise from our lives as much as we can that is petty and meretricious and that we open our hearts to the suffering of this world, imbuing our art with as luminous and compassionate a spirit as we can.

—Steve Kowit, from the introduction to his book
In the Palm of Your Hand: The Poet's Portable Workshop

Kowit's poetry and essays appear in numerous journals, and his poems have been read by Garrison Keillor on NPR. Influenced by 19th-century American poets Walt Whitman and Hart Crane, as well as by 20th-century poets such as Alan Ginsberg and Jorie Graham, Kowit's writing possesses an unabashed social consciousness. That he was raised in a Zionist family may explain in part why his writing is intensely spiritual as well as polemic—aptly captured in poems like "Intifada," and in articles such as "The Mass Suicide of the Xhosa: A Study in Collective Self-Deception," which examines genocidal colonialism and was published in *Skeptic* magazine (Volume 11, No. 1).

With one exception ("202 East 7th," which was first published in *The California Journal of Poetics*), the poems in this first portfolio are reprinted from three of his collections: *The Dumbbell Nebula, The Gods of Rapture,* and *The First Noble Truth.*

The Blue Dress

When I grab big Eddie, the gopher drops from his teeth
& bolts for the closet, vanishing
into a clutter of shoes & valises & vacuum
attachments, & endless boxes of miscellaneous rubbish.
Grumbling & cursing, carton by carton,
I lug everything out:
that mountain of hopeless detritus—until,
with no place to hide, he breaks
for the other side of the room & I have him at last,
trapped in a corner, tiny & trembling.
I lower the plastic freezer bowl over his head &
         Boom!—
slam the thing down.
       "Got him!" I yell out,
slipping a folder under the edge for a lid.
But when I open the front door, it's teeming,
a rain so fierce it drives me back into the house,
& before I can wriggle into my sneakers,
Mary, impatient, has grabbed the contraption
out of my hands & run off into the yard with it, barefoot.
She's wearing that blue house dress.
I know just where she's headed: that big
mossy boulder down by the oleanders
across from the shed,
& I know what she'll do when she gets there—hunker
down, slip off the folder,
let the thing slide to the ground
while she speaks to him softly, whispers
encouraging, comforting things.
Only after the gopher takes a few tentative steps,
dazed, not comprehending how he got back
to his own world, then tries to run off,
will she know how he's fared: if he's wounded,

or stunned, or okay—depraved ravisher
of our gladiolus & roses, but neighbor & kin nonetheless.
Big Eddie meows at my feet while I stand
by the window over the sink, watching
her run back thru the rain,
full of good news. Triumphant. Laughing. Wind
lashing the trees. It's hard to fathom
how gorgeous she looks, running like that
through the storm: that blue
sheath of a dress aglow in the smokey haze—
that luminous blue dress pasted by rain to her hips.
I stand at the window grinning, amazed
at my own undeserved luck—
at a life that I still, when I think of it, hardly believe.

[Editor's Note: Steve and Mary had been married 48 years at the time of his death. Not surprisingly, this poem was an audience favorite. See also "Steve Kowit Reads 'The Blue Dress,'" a YouTube video shot at Ducky Waddles Emporium Book Store in 2011:

https://www.youtube.com/watch?v=h5m-EUft_uU]

A Trick

Late afternoon. Huancayo. We'd made the long haul
down from Ayacucho that morning. Were hungry & tired. Had stumbled
into one of those huge, operatic, down-at-the-heels Peruvian
restaurants: teardrop chandeliers, candles
in ribbed silver cages, frayed red cloths on the tables.
A building of three red brick walls & one of that massive, grey,
mortarless, hand-hewn stone whose secret had died with the Incas.
Not a soul in the place but a sleepy middle-aged waiter
tricked out in the shabby black & white jacket & slacks
of the trade. He brought us two menus, goblets for wine,
& a plate of *papas a la Huancaina.*
I was unaccountably happy. In one of those silly, insouciant moods
that come out of nowhere, despite the fact that the planet
was falling apart all around us. The previous summer
I'd given the Army the slip, leaving to better men than myself
the task of carpet-bombing the indigent peasants of Asia.
We'd exchanged matrimonial vows in Seattle & then headed south.
Had been bussing for months from town to town thru the Andes.
The truth is, the whole thing had happened by magic. "Hey,
you know the trick where you blow an invisible coin
into a sealed-up glass?" I lowered a saucer over her long
stemmed goblet so nothing could enter, & grinned
as if I were going to pluck out of nowhere fishes & loaves.
Mary said No, she didn't—& laughed, preparing herself
for another fine piece of buffoonery. On the table between us,
though it wasn't yet dark, the candle was already lit.
In the distance, the endless sierra. I asked her to hand me
a coin, placed it into my palm, recited some hocus-pocus
known only to shamans from Brooklyn, then spread
out my fingers, & lo & behold it had vanished!
So far so good. But that part was easy. What I did next
was harder—to blow that invisible coin into the sealed-up glass.
The nice thing was you could see it fall in with a clatter,

hear the luxurious clink of silver in glass as it dropped
out of nowhere & settled. Needless to say, she was amazed.
I mean *really* amazed! & so too, as it turns out, was our waiter,
who'd been watching the whole affair from the wall by the kitchen,
& flew to my side, flailing his arms like a sinner whose soul
the Holy Spirit had entered—& who knows he is saved.
He wanted to know how I'd done it. How such a thing
could possibly happen. *Milagro!* I felt like Jesus
raising the dead: a little embarrassed, but pleased
that I'd brought the thing off—& that someone had seen it.
Huancayo. I liked the looks of the place. That sharp
mountain light before dusk. Folks walking around
on the other side of the window in woolen serapes.
If it wouldn't have sounded so pious, or grandiose,
I'd have said to that fellow: "Friend, how I did it
really isn't the point; in this world nothing is more or less
amazing than anything else." But I didn't. Instead,
I just shrugged, the way that when Lazarus opened his eyes
& shook off the dust & put on his hat, Jesus himself
must have shrugged, as much as to say it was nothing, a trifle.
The three of us chatted a bit & then we checked
out the menus & ordered the meal we'd come in for—me
& Mary, my wife, all wit & forbearance & grace,
who one day had fallen by some sort of miracle into my life.

[Editor's Note: In 1996, this poem was the Grand Prize Winner in the
Atlanta Review International Poetry Competition.]

[From *The Gods of Rapture*]

If she denies it she is lying—
there were witnesses:
two purple gallinules
among the spatterdock;
a heron,
standing motionless
on one long
reed-like leg;
& silver minnows
leaping
in the moon-drenched waters.

    after Kapilar

Metaphysics

The trouble with me is I have a low metaphysical threshold.
When I'm told the bicameral mind can never know things in themselves,
I shake my head gravely. . .but simply out of politeness.
Frankly, the conflict between the noumenal & phenomenal worlds
means nothing to me whatsoever.
Is perceptual knowledge constrained by the categorical space
in which language unfolds,
or is Absolute Is-ness provoked by the Relative Ought?
"Well, I'd never quite thought of things in that light. . . ."
I stammer & cough. I help myself to the cheese dip.
Perhaps I'm obtuse, but I could never recall whether it's Essence
that precedes Existence, or the other way round.
The fact is I'd rather my pinky get slammed in the door of a semi
than argue over the epistemological underpinnings of post-deconstruction
whether signifiers are self-referential, or meaning culture-specific.
It's knotty alright, I say, stifling a yawn.
The question of course is who is that redhead,
the one at the other end of the room with the lavender
lipstick & radical décolletage?
& why at these awful soirees do I always get stuck among the professors?
If it isn't free will, they are beating to death the mind-body dilemma,
the transcendental nature of Time, that gut-wrenching issue:
does or does not the external world really exist?
Ah, now she is crossing her legs!
I help myself to the pretzels. I pour some more wine.
Let them build the City of God out of earwax & toothpicks without me.
And what, pray tell, is the meaning of Meaning?
Are Existence & Nothingness one & the same?
And how in the Bright Night of Dread does the body of Ontic Being arise?
I shake my head, as much as to say I too am perplexed.
Politeness itself, I am loathe to point out that perhaps what we need
is more daylight & less metaphysics.
As if this world isn't perfectly real as it is, or as real as it gets,

they want us to think that the world behind it is better,
that the dead are elsewhere & happy,
that our loved ones are waiting for us on the other side of *samsara*.
As if that sort of cerebral monoxide could stifle
the groans of the dying, the winds of disaster, the weeping
that's left here behind us. & still they go on.
Armageddon itself would not be enough to dissuade them!
Is Spirit immortal? Do dreams occupy space?
Is the universe purposeful, random, unbounded, autogenous, finite, alive?
Is death an illusion? Or simply another sort of beginning?
A journey indeed—but whither & whence?
Yes, yes! I say, my head spinning.
It's utterly fascinating! Who would have guessed it!
Far off in the night, a coyote howls at the moon.
I have by now finished the cheese dip, the pretzels, the wine.
The lickerish redhead has long since slipped off
on the arms of her lover—some young, good-looking swine.
I rise with a hundred regrets, thanking my hosts,
zipping my jacket, & spouting farewells in every direction:
It's certainly something to ponder, I tell them,
but really, I have to get going.
It's late & tomorrow I'm up bright and early.
A marvelous evening! Your quiche by the way was divine!

The Prodigal Son's Brother

who'd been steadfast as small change all his life
forgave the one who bounced back like a bad check
the moment his father told him he ought to.
After all, that's what being good means.
In fact, it was he who hosted the party,
bought the crepes & champagne,
uncorked every bottle. With each drink
another toast to his brother: ex-swindler, hit-man
& rapist. By the end of the night
the entire village was blithering drunk
in an orgy of hugs & forgiveness,
while he himself,
whose one wish was to be loved as profusely,
slipped in & out of their houses,
stuffing into a satchel their brooches & rings
& bracelets & candelabra.
Then lit out at dawn with a light heart
for a port city he knew only by reputation:
ladies in lipstick hanging out of each window,
& every third door a saloon.

202 East 7th

Now & again I catch myself staring back into that world,
decades gone. Cassidy is defending the Chinese
Revolution, arms crossed over his lean, naked chest.
He is 20, agitated of course, but laughing, nevertheless,
as he paces the room. From a chair in the corner,
Doug Reisner's hoarse, equivocal chuckle, & Lenny
is grinning, delighted, & Murray, laconic as ever, nodding
his head. That quiet, measured womanly voice is Susan
Hartung's. Outside, the blazing white impossible glare
from the street, & more dimly lit than I guess it must really
have been, the narrow, endless tenement stairway I climb
to that earlier life, in this waking dream, again & again.

A Betrayal

A friend I hadn't seen in more than three decades wrote
to tell me he had just remarried & was finally happy;
this followed by a long denunciation of his former wife,
whom I had known back then when all of us were young,
& who, through tireless manipulation & deceit (or so
he claimed), had won full custody of the kids,
thus ruining two decades of his life. "She wouldn't
even show me the room where they slept," he wrote,
"or offer me a cup of water from the kitchen tap."
I was shocked, though at the same time could not help
but think back to that afternoon a few weeks
after their first son's birth when my friend had dropped by,
exuberantly happy, & in the midst of kidding about how
little sleep they were getting, mentioned, in passing,
that they had taken Sasha, their lovable Irish setter,
back to the pound: "With an infant in the house. . ." he started
to explain—the way one might about a troublesome TV
or a sofabed returned for taking up too much space in the den.
I stood there stunned. "But. . .why. . .didn't you find her another
home?" I tried to keep my voice under control.
"You know as well as I do at those places only puppies
get adopted. She'll. . .she'll be put down."
It came out broken. I could hardly wrap my mouth
about the words. "Oh, not at all," he laughed. "Sasha's
so adorable she's bound to find a family that will take her in!"
He shook his head with a dismissive grin & then went on
about the endless pleasures of his infant son, & I said
nothing further. What more, I'd like to know, could I have said?
By the time I was done reading his letter, the sun had set.
I sat there for a long moment, then read it through
a second time, trying, this time, to be as careful as I could
not to betray our friendship, to keep in mind what a fine,
decent, well-intentioned fellow he had always been, & all

that he had evidently suffered. Though it didn't work. Sasha
kept pacing back and forth across the cage of that
disquieting letter, pausing now & then to lick the back
of my right hand. She could not comprehend what had happened.
Had she done something wrong? Where were those humans
she had loved so much, those humans who had seemed
so trustworthy & generous & kind? I folded up his letter,
set it down, & watched through the west window bands
of violet & magenta spread across the summer dusk & darken.
Try as I might, however earnestly I wished him well in his new life,
it smolders in me still—that old, unspoken, unforgiving anger.

Will Boland & I

stroll from Dog Beach down to Cape May, grumbling
over this nation's inexhaustible
predilection for carnage: the mask of rectitude
painted over the skull of vindictive rage.
It is midwinter, the beach all but deserted:
an elderly gent walks an elderly golden retriever;
a family of four is out hunting for shells;
two good old boys chugging their Michelobs
take in the last of the sunset:
down at their feet, Iwo Jimaed into the sand,
a colossal American flag
that they've lugged down here to the beach
with their cooler of beer to cheer on the home team.
Night & day, on the other side of the world,
daisy-cutters are pounding a village
to shambles, bathing the landscape in blood.
Women crouch in the rubble rocking their dead.
                    —*Listen,* I say to Will.
E. O. Wilson can swear up & down there are species
of ants even more compulsively homicidal
than man; I, for one, remain unconvinced.

Above us, that gorgeous midwinter dusk.
At our feet, the Pacific, ablaze in magentas & red.
True enough, he ventures, *but Steve, you've got*
to admit we're just as much a part of this world
as anything else. . .& maybe,
in some crazy way, marvelous too!
                    I shrug.
We walk on in silence.
A couple of high school girls,
frolicking in & out of the surf, smile up at us sweetly.
                    A part of this world, yes, I snarl back.

But surely the ugliest part!—the words hardly
out of my mouth when those two young women,
now twenty yards or so down the beach,
suddenly fling open their arms, rise to their toes,
leap into the air, & float there—angelic. . .unearthly. . .
impossibly luminous creatures, alighting
at last in a dazzle of pirouettes & glissades,
only to rise up into the air again & again, while Will
& I stand there—dumbfounded, grinning, amazed.
Under the flare of the night's first stars
each *grande jete* more splendid, rapturous,
vaulting! Two ardently schooled young ballerinas,
silhouetted against the indigo flames
of the darkening western horizon.
The last of the light of this world setting behind them.

The Black Shoe

A couple of newlyweds, up at the Del Mar station,
saw the woman stumble & fall, & ran back
to pull her to safety, the train bearing down.
For a thousand feet north of the point of impact,
investigators found parts of a briefcase, sketches
of gowns, a low-heeled black shoe. From
the White House, the President screaming for blood.
A quarter million American boys already shipped
to the Gulf. No doubt some of the kids
from the base: Mike Santos & Tracy & Kevin, horsing
around like they used to in class—a football
spiraling over the Saudi Arabian sands. At night,
unable to sleep, tossing in bed, I hatch extravagant plots
to bring the ship of state down. I am determined
that not a single one of my students shall die;
not a single Iraqi infant be orphaned
or murdered. Such are the feverish thoughts
that spin through my head in that fugue state
before sleep lifts me out of myself & carries me off.
In the morning, however, it isn't the President
circled by microphones screeching for war
that throbs in my head, but that unstoppable train
& the fact that both women were killed: the one
who'd just gotten married, reaching her arms
to the arms of the one who had stumbled
& fallen. It won't let me rest. That briefcase.
Those bloody sketches of gowns. The black shoe.

[From *The Gods of Rapture*]

Let the flame of my passion
glow in the eyes of my beloved.
Let it illuminate our path.
Let the liquid
of which our bodies are composed
be at once the river refreshing us
& the well
at which we quench our thirst.
Let our spirits be the air
we breathe
& thru which we move
till we are no longer ourselves,
& I lie by my beloved's side
in the earth.
Let our dusts be one.

    after Govindadasa

Second Portfolio:
Ten Poems from *Lurid Confessions*

T. S. Eliot was perfectly right when he said that a poet, while in the act of composing, works as a musician. Always and everywhere the music of the poem is the decisive factor. But I love the power of the story, too, which is, at its deepest level, a vehicle for expressing the inexpressible . . . .

What do I want from my poems? I guess I want to move the reader with memorable tales that celebrate the whole inexplicable business— this strange, unspeakably marvelous life. That's what poems do at their best.

—from *Steve Kowit Greatest Hits 1978–2003*

World-class award-winning poet, teacher, and activist Steve Kowit continues to be "a major figure in poetry in America today," as Duff Brenna, Founding Editor of *Serving House Journal*, says. "He was also the best lecturer and commentator on the craft of creative writing that I've ever seen in action."

Lurid Confessions, Kowit's first full-length poetry collection, had two printings with Carpenter Press, one in 1983 and the other in 1984, but had been out of print ever since—until 2010.

"It's been our loss not to have access to the wit and insights of so many excellent poems," said the editors at Serving House Books. They were proud to publish a new soft-cover edition of the book, released in July 2010.

"Treat yourself," says Brenna, "take a look and be prepared to shake your head in wonder. Kowit is brilliant, but he also has a UNIQUE sense of humor that will have you rolling with laughter."

The title poem of *Lurid Confessions* is also reprinted in *Stand Up Poetry: The Poetry of Los Angeles and Beyond* (Red Wind Books, 1990), edited by Charles Harper Webb and Suzanne Lummis. In a footnote to the poem, the editors describe Kowit and other poets included in the anthology as not so much favoring performance over print as moving "away from the dour and ponderous, toward creativity, spontaneity, and childlike (not childish) joy."

An Introduction by Steve Kowit
[29 March 2010]

[. . .] This past February, at the invitation of Ricki Rycraft, I did a reading at Mt. San Jacinto College and afterwards we sat around at Ricki's house in Menifee with Duff Brenna and Clyde Fixmer, old friends from the days when Duff, Clyde, and I taught together at San Diego State University. Ricki's a short story writer, Clyde's a poet, and in 1990 Duff published *The Book of Mamie* to rave reviews, a profoundly moving novel that knocked me off my feet. He's written half a dozen splendid novels since.

The four of us were chatting and laughing when Duff mentioned that he owned a copy of *Lurid Confessions*. I was shocked, shocked that he even knew of the book, let alone owned a copy. I mentioned offhandedly that for years I'd been wanting to send that long-forgotten book, my first full collection of poems, out in the mails again on the off chance that some press might be willing to reprint it. Duff was immediately interested. He said it was a book he'd always liked a good deal and that he might be able to help. I could see from his face that a happy idea was brewing. Two days later I got an email from him and another one from Tom Kennedy (another terrific novelist), and a third email from Walter Cummins, novelist, short story writer and Editor Emeritus of *The Literary Review*. Walter had been kind enough, years ago, to publish in *The Literary Review* "Stolen Kisses," an essay of mine about the pleasures and hazards of literary cross-fertilization. He had recently started a publishing venture, Serving House Books, and asked me to send him, on Duff and Tom's recommendation, a copy of the book. So that's how *Lurid Confessions* got its second life. I am enormously grateful to all of them for having urged these poems back into the world.

For that original 1983 edition, I conceived the silly cover art, Bodhidharma and lady friend. (Michael Previte, if you're out there somewhere in this world, thanks for that charming drawing!) But in the original Carpenter Press version it was mistakenly printed sideways, an annoying error that I fixed by printing up a wrap-around paper cover with the art sitting the way it should. Needless to say, I'm delighted to see that error corrected. My beloved wife Mary's frontispiece, that equally silly drawing of Madame Blavatsky as a young girl, is also from the original edition. It's based on an illustration she found in a Mexican comic book. I still nod my head at the epigram from Henry Miller and still find the one from the Amida Sutra heartbreakingly true, and I still think the blurbs on the back cover make precisely the statement the book wants. And that old snapshot of me also on the back cover will do well enough: like the poems themselves, it's a younger and somewhat lighter-of-spirit version of who I am now. As for the poems, I've cleaned up some of the punctuation, corrected three spelling errors, reversed two lines, and changed a couple of words. Other than that the poems are as they originally appeared.

There is nothing much more that needs to be said. I am, of course, delighted that you are holding *Lurid Confessions* in your hands. My hope is that some of these poems will touch you or make you smile or bring you back with some small jolt to your own life, and that whatever time you devote to this little book will not be poorly spent.

For Mary,
for my friends,
in loving memory of my parents,
& for you.

Blue things are blue, red things are red. . . .
That is what we call Paradise.
—Amida Sutra

I expect the angels to piss in my beer.
—Henry Miller

Mysteries

Tonight, sick with the flu & alone, I drift
in confusion & neurasthenia surrendering
to the chaos & mystery of all things,
for tonight it comes to me like a sad but obvious revelation
that we know nothing at all.
Despite all our fine theories we don't have the foggiest
notion of why or how anything in this world exists
or what anything means or how anything fits
or what we or anyone else are doing here in the first place.
Tonight the whole business is simply beyond me.
Painfully I sit up in bed & look out the window
into the evening. There is a light on
in Marie's apartment. My neighbor Marie, the redhead,
is moving away. She found a cheaper apartment elsewhere.
She is packing up her belongings.
The rest of the street is dark, bereft.
In this world, nothing is ruled out & nothing is certain:
a savage carnivorous primate bloated with arrogance
floating about on a tiny island
among the trillions of islands out in the darkness.
Did you know that the human brain was larger 40 millennia back?
Does that mean they were smarter?
It stands to reason they were but we simply don't know.
& what of the marriage dance of the scorpion?
Do whales breach from exuberance
or for some sort of navigational reason?
What does the ant queen know or do to provoke such undying devotion?
What of the coelacanth & the Neopilina—
not a fossil trace for 300 million years
then one day there she is swimming around.
In the mangrove swamps the fruit-bats hang from the trees
& flutter their great black wings.
How does a turnip sprout from a seed?

Creatures that hatch out of eggs & walk about on the earth
as if of their own volition.
How does a leaf unwind on its stem & turn red in the fall
& drop like a feather onto the snowy fields of the spinning world?
What does the shaman whisper into the ear of the beetle
that the beetle repeats to the rain?
Why does the common moth so love the light
she is willing to die? Is it some incurable hunger for warmth?
At least that I can understand.
How & why does the salmon swim thousands of miles back
to find the precise streambed, the very rock
under which it was born? God knows what that urge is
to be home in one's bed if only to die. There have been dogs,
abandoned by families moving to other parts of the country
who have followed thru intricate cities,
over the wildest terrain —exhausted & bloody & limping—
a trail that in no way could be said to exist,
to scratch at a door it had never seen,
months, in cases even years, later.
Events such as these cannot be explained. If indeed
we are made of the same stuff as sea kelp & stars,
what that stuff is we haven't any idea.
The very atom eludes us.
Is it a myth & the cosmos an infinite series of Chinese boxes,
an onion of unending minusculation?
What would it look like apart from the grid of the language—
cut loose from its names?
Is there no solid ground upon which to plant our molecular flag?
What of the microorganic civilizations
living their complex domestic histories out in the roots of our hair?
Is there life in the stars?
Are there creatures like us weeping in furnished rooms
out past the solar winds in the incalculable dark
where everything's spinning away from everything else?
Are we just configurations of energy pulsing in space?
As if that explained this!
Is the universe conscious? Have we lived other lives?

Does the spirit exist? Is it immortal?
Do these questions even make sense?
& all this weighs on me like a verdict of exile.
I brush back the curtain an inch.
It flutters, as if by some ghostly hand.
Now Marie's light is off & the world is nothing again,
utterly vacant, sunyata, the indecipherable void. How awesome
& sad & mysterious everything is tonight.
Tell me this, was the Shroud of Turin really the deathshroud of Jesus?
What of those tears that gush from the wounds
of particular icons? Don't tell me they don't;
thousands of people have seen them.
Did Therese Newman really survive on a wafer a day?
& the levitations of Eusapia Pallachino & St. Teresa.
& Salsky who suffered the stigmata in that old Victorian house
on Oak Street across from the Panhandle
on Good Friday. With my own eyes I saw them—his palms full of blood.
Where does everything disappear that I loved?
The old friends with whom I would wander about
lost in rhapsodic babble, stoned, in the dark:
Jim Fraser, Guarino, Steve Parker & Mednick & Burke—
squabbling & giggling over the cosmos. That walk-up
on 7th Street overlooking the tenement roofs of Manhattan.
Lovely Elizabeth dead & Ronnie OD'd on a rooftop in Brooklyn
& Jerry killed in the war & the women—those dark,
furtive kisses & sighs; all the mysterious moanings of sex.
Where did I lose the addresses of all those people I knew?
Now even their names are gone: taken, lost, abandoned,
vanished into the blue. Where is the OED
I won at Brooklyn College for writing a poem
& the poem itself decades gone, & the black & gold Madison
High School tennis team captain's jacket I was so proud of?
Where is that beaded headband? The marvelous Indian flute?
That book of luminous magic-marker paintings Eliot did?
& where is Eliot now? & Greg Marquez? & Marvin Torfield?
Where are the folding scissors from Avenida Abancay in Lima?
Where is the antique pocket watch Rosalind Eichenstein gave me:

I loved it so—the painted shepherd playing the flute
in the greenest, most minuscule hills.
I bet some junkie on 7th Street took it
but there's no way now to find out. It just disappeared
& no one & nothing that's lost will ever be back.
How came a cuneiform tablet unearthed by the Susquehanna?
Why was Knossos never rebuilt?
What blast flattened the Tunguska forest in 1908?
& those things that fall from the sky—manna
from heaven & toads & huge blocks of ice & alabaster
& odd-shaped gelatinous matter—fafrotskis
of every description & type
that at one time or another have fallen out of the sky?
The alleged Venezuelan fafrotski—what is it exactly
& where did it come from?
& quarks & quasars & black holes. . . . The woolly mammoth,
one moment peacefully grazing on clover in sunlight,
an instant later quick-frozen into the arctic
antediluvian north. What inconceivable cataclysm occurred?
How did it happen?
What would my own children have looked like?
Why is there always one shoe on the freeway?
Why am I shivering? What am I even doing
writing this poem? Is it all nothing but ego—my name
screaming out from the grave?
I look out the window again. How strange,
now the tobacco shop on the corner is lit.
A gaunt, mustachioed figure steps to the doorway & looks at my window
& waves. Why, it's Fernando Pessoa!
I wave back—Fernando! Fernando! I cry out.
But he doesn't see me. He can't. The light snaps off.
The tobacco shop disappears into the blackness, into the past. . . .
Who was the ghost in the red cape who told Henry IV he would die?
What of those children raised by wolves & gazelles?
What of spontaneous human combustion—those people
who burst into flame? Is space really curved?
Did the universe have a beginning

or did some sort of primal matter always exist?
Either way it doesn't make sense!
How does the pion come tumbling out of the void
& where does it vanish once it is gone?
& we too—into what & where do we vanish?
For the worms, surely we too are meat on the hoof.
Frankly it scares me, it scares the hell out of me.
The back of my neck is dripping with sweat. . .a man
with a fever located somewhere along the Pacific Coast
in the latter half of the 20th century by the Julian calendar:
a conscious, momentary configuration; a bubble in the stew;
a child of the dark. I am going to stand up now if I can,
—that's what I'm going to do—
& make my way to the kitchen
& find the medicine Mary told me was there.
Perhaps she was right. Perhaps it will help me to sleep.
Yes, that's what I'll do, I'll sleep & forget.
We know only the first words of the message—if that.
I could weep when I think of how lovely it was
in its silver case all engraved with some sort of floral design,
the antique watch that Rosalind gave me years ago
on the Lower East Side of Manhattan
when we were young & in love & had nothing but time—that watch
with its little shepherd playing a flute on the tiny hillside,
gone now like everything else.
Where in the name of Christ did it disappear to—
that's what I want to know!

Hate Mail

I got a letter from an old acquaintance in New York
asking me to send some of my prose poems
to her literary magazine, *Unhinged.*
I should have known better.
In the old days she'd fluttered about
the coffee houses baring her long teeth.
We'd smile up politely and cover our throats.
But time makes you forget & ambition got the better of me
& a week later I got my poems back with a terse note:
Sorry, but this third-rate pornographic crap isn't for us.
& may I point out it is presumptuous of you
not to have enclosed a self-addressed stamped envelope.
Just who in hell does little Stevie Kowit think he is?
I was nonplussed.
I sent a stamp back with a note explaining
that I hadn't thought I was submitting to her magazine
so much as answering her letter.
I received a blistering reply:
Who was I kidding? What I had sent was a submission
to *Unhinged,* pure & simple.
In passing she referred to me as juvenile,
adolescent, immature, a sniveling brat, an infant
& a little baby—
truly the letter of a raving lunatic.
I suppose it would have been best to have ignored it,
forget the whole thing,
but that little Stevie Kowit business started eating at me,
so I dropped a one-liner in an envelope & sent it off:
Dear C, you are a ca-ca pee-pee head.

It Was Your Song

I saw her once, briefly,
in the park
among the folk musicians
twenty years ago—
a barefoot child of twelve
or thirteen
in a light serape
& the faded, skintight Levis
of the era. I recall
exactly how she stood there:
one foot on the rise
of the fountain
finger-picking that guitar
& singing
in the most alluring
& delicious voice,
& as she sang she'd
flick her hair
behind one shoulder
in a gesture that meant nothing,
yet I stood there
stunned.
One of those exquisite
creatures of the Village
who would hang around
Rienzi's & Folk City,
haunting all the coffee houses
of MacDougal Street,
that child
has haunted my life
for twenty years.
Forgive me.
I am myself reticent

to speak of it,
this embarrassing infatuation
for a young girl,
seen once, briefly,
decades back,
as I hurried thru the park.
But there it is.
& I have written this
that I might linger at her side
a moment longer,
& to praise the Alexandrian,
Cavafy, that devotee
of beautiful boys
& shameless rhapsodist
of the ephemeral encounter.
Cavafy, it was your song
from which I borrowed
both the manner & the courage.

Wanted—Sensuous Woman Who Can Handle 12 Inches of Man

From an ad in the Miami Phoenix

She was sensuous to a fault
& perfectly willing
though somewhat taken aback.
In fact, at first,
she noticed no one at the door at all.
"Down here!. . .down here!. . ."
I shrieked.
—Need I add that once again
I left unsatisfied.

Kowit

Sometimes when I'm not there to defend myself
the friends start playing *Kowit.*
Right from the start, the game,
begun with what seemed nothing
if not innocent affection,
takes a nasty turn:
from quietly amused to openly derisive,
ruthless, scathing, & at last
maniacally sadistic—
a psychopathic bacchanal of innuendo,
malice & vindictive lies.
It's jealousy & spite is what it is of course.
They're rankled by my talent & integrity,
the editors & fancy women who surround me.
So Kowit's torn upon the rack
& barbecued alive
& chewed out of his skin like a salami
till there is nothing left of him
but blood & phlegm & scat
& fingernails & teeth
& the famous Kowit penis
which is passed about the room
to little squeals of laughter,
like a ridiculous hat.

Lurid Confessions

One fine morning they move in for the pinch
& snap on the cuffs—just like that.
Turns out they've known all about you for years,
have a file the length of a paddy-wagon
with everything—tapes, prints, film. . .
the whole shmear. Don't ask me how but
they've managed to plug a mike into one of your molars
& know every felonious move & transgression
back to the very beginning, with ektachromes
of your least indiscretion & peccadillo.
Needless to say, you are thrilled,
though sitting there in the docket
you bogart it, tough as an old tooth—
your jaw set, your sleeves rolled
& three days of stubble. . . . Only,
when they play it back it looks different:
a life common & loathsome as gum stuck to a chair.
Tedious hours of you picking your nose,
scratching, eating, clipping your toenails. . . .
Alone, you look stupid; in public, your rapier
wit is slimy & limp as an old band-aid.
They have thousands of pictures of people around you
stifling yawns. As for sex—a bit
of pathetic groping among the unlovely & luckless:
a dance with everyone making steamy love in the dark
& you alone in a corner eating a pretzel.
You leap to your feet protesting
that's not how it was, they have it all wrong.
But nobody hears you. The bailiff
is snoring, the judge is cleaning his teeth,
the jurors are all wearing glasses with eyes painted open.
The flies have folded their wings & stopped buzzing.
In the end, after huge doses of coffee,

the jury is polled. One after another
they manage to rise to their feet
like narcoleptics in August, sealing your fate:
Innocent... innocent... innocent.... Right down the line.
You are carried out screaming.

The Poetry Reading Was a Disaster

& I had expected so much.
All the big kahunas would be there—
the New York literati & foundation honchos
& publishing magi & hordes of insouciant groupies
& millions of poets—
the shaggy vanguard in green Adidas snapping their fingers,
surrealists whirling about by the ceiling
like adipose St. Teresas in mufti,
Bolinas cowboys & tatterdemalion beatniks
& Buddhists with mandarin beards & big goofy eyes
& Iowa poets in blazers & beanies
& Poundians nodding gigantic foreheads.
What tumultuous applause would erupt when I stepped
to the stage. What a thunder of adoration!
The room would be shaking.
The very city would tremble.
The whole damn Pacific Plate start to shudder.
One good jolt & everything west of the San Andreas
would squirt back into Mesopotamian waters
& this time for good—
jesus but they would love me! . . . .
Except when I got to the place it was tiny,
a hole in the wall,
& only a handful had shown up
& as soon as I walked to the front of the room
a kid started whining,
a chap in the second row fell asleep
& a trashed-out punk rocker with a swastika t-shirt,
drool on his chin & arms down to his knees
started cackling out loud. The razor blade
chained at his throat bounced up & down.
Somewhere a couple must have been screwing around
under their seats—I heard tongues

lapping it up, orgasmic weeping,
groans that grew louder and louder.
The kid wouldn't shut up.
The sleeper started to snore.
Potato chip eaters in every direction
were groping around in tinfoil bags
while the poetry lover, my host,
was oohing & aahing in all the wrong places.
I looked up politely. Couldn't they please,
please be a little more quiet.
Somebody snickered. There was a slap
& the brat started to bawl.
Someone stormed out in a huff slamming the door.
Another screamed that I was a pig & a sexist.
A heavy-set lady in thick Mensa glasses leaped to her feet
& announced that she was a student of Mark Strand.
In the back, the goon with the tattooed shirt
& the blade was guffawing & flapping his wings.
What could I do?
I read for all I was worth, straight from the heart,
all duende & dazzle—
no one & nothing was going to stop me!
Inspired at last, I read to a room
that had fallen utterly silent.
They must have been awed.
I wailed to the winds like Cassandra,
shoring our language against the gathering dark.
I raged at the heavens themselves
& ended the last set in tears, on my knees. . . .
When I looked up it was night & I was alone
except for an old lady up on a stepladder
scrubbing what looked like glops of shit off the wall
& humming.
The place stank of ammonia.
Thank you so much
had been scribbled over my briefcase in lipstick
or blood. Someone had stepped on my glasses,

lifted my wallet,
& sliced off all of my buttons,
half of my mustache,
& one of my balls.

Cutting Our Losses

In a downtown San Jose hotel,
exhausted & uptight & almost broke,
we blew 16 *colónes* & got stewed on rum.
You lounged in bed
reading *Hermelinda Linda* comics
while I stumbled drunk around the room
complaining
& reciting poems out of an old anthology.
I read that Easter elegy of Yeats'
which moved you,
bringing back that friend of yours,
Bob Fishman, who was dead.
You wept. I felt terrible.
We killed the bottle, made a blithered
kind of love & fell asleep.
Out in the Costa Rican night
the weasels of the dark held a fiesta
celebrating our safe arrival in their city
& our sound sleep.
We found our Ford Econoline next
morning where we'd left it,
on a side street, but ripped
apart like a piñata,
like a tortured bird, wing
window busted in, a door
sprung open on its pins like an astonished beak.
Beloved, everything we lost—our old blues
tapes, the telephoto lens, the Mayan priest,
that ancient Royal Portable I loved—
awoke me to how tentative & delicate
& brief & precious it all is, & was
for that a sort of aphrodisiac—though bitter
to swallow. That evening,

drunk on loss, I loved you
wildly, with a crazy passion, knowing
as I did, at last, the secret
of your own quietly voluptuous heart—you
who have loved always with a desperation
born as much of sorrow as of lust,
being, I suppose, at once unluckier,
& that much wiser to begin with.

Out of McHenry

Broken fence thru the mist.
Bitter fruit of the wild pear
& vines full of berries.
The stone path
buried in brambles
& mud
& the shack in ruins,
rotted thru
like an old crate:
half the roof caved in.
The whole place
gone to weed & debris.
Someone before me
sick of his life
must have figured this
was as far as he'd get
& nailed it up
out in the void,
then died here
or left
decades ago.
A swallow
skitters among the beams
& flies out
thru the open frame of a window.
Now nothing inhabits the place
but tin cans
covered with webs,
a mattress,
a handful of tools
busted and useless—
& myself
where he stood

here in the doorway,
in mist,
high up over this world.
Trees & flowers dripping with cold rain.

Crossing the River

I am translating a poem by Domingo Alfonso
called "Crossing the River."
When I lift my head from the page it is night.
I walk thru the rooms aware of the shapes
that loom in the silence.
In the bedroom, Mary has fallen asleep.
I stand in the doorway & watch her breathing
& wonder what it will be like
when one of us dies.
In 8 years
we have not been apart for more than a few days.
The cat drops to my feet & sashays past me.
I open the side door. Outside
there is no sound whatsoever. If things
call to each other at this hour of night
I do not hear them. Vega alone
gleams overhead, thousands of light years
off in the region of Lyra.
The great harp is still.

Selected Essays and Reviews

Stolen Kisses

Several years ago Dorianne Laux called from Petaluma to read me a poem that she was working on called "Kissing." It was terrific. She could hear the pleasure in my voice when I told her how much I liked it. It was one of those splendid pieces that was bound to find its way into any number of anthologies. But what I didn't tell her, what I suppressed, because it would have sounded tacky and accusatory, was that what she had read me was my own goddam poem! Once, years earlier, when we were both living in San Diego, I had talked to her about a long piece I was taking notes for, about a couple kissing while the panorama of history, the endless bloodletting of *Homo satanicus,* unfolded behind them. And that was exactly what Dorianne had done: "They are still kissing when the cars crash and the bombs drop, when the babies are born crying into the white air, when Mozart bends to his bowl of soup and Stalin bends to his garden." Yes! Exactly! Just what I'd had in mind.

Of course, she hadn't the slightest recollection that her idea had come from that conversation, and there seemed no point in mentioning it. Besides, stealing ideas for poems is what poets do as a matter of course. At least, it's what I do. Even in poems written directly out of my own experience I am apt to use notions, phrases and musical ideas filched from other writers—Dorianne Laux certainly among them. Into one recent poem—a poem about the pleasures of poetic lineage—I incorporate a *tanka* by Izumi Shikibu (inspired by Jane Hirshfield's lovely translation); then I steal an image from Ray Carver, quote Eliot, and end with a line from Pound. To ice the cake, its title, "Madness and Civilization," was snitched from Foucault. No less egregiously, I've published two books of "imitations" of *srngararasa,* the erotic-mood poetry of India—poems made up of situations lifted whole cloth from that ancient tradition and then shamelessly reworked into my own idiom. Allen Ginsberg once told me with great pleasure that his poem "Things I Don't Know" came out of my long poem "Mysteries," a poem that was itself inspired by Fernando Pessoa's "Tobacco Shop" and, even more directly, by Ben Belitt's luscious translation of Pablo Neruda's "Los Enigmas." Oddly, I didn't realize I had stolen Neruda's idea till one day, years later, I started rereading his poem and was shocked. Even my title was outright larceny!

After that phone call with Dorianne I decided to reclaim my kiss poem, that is to say, to do a version of my own, for the ambitious one of years before had never materialized. I don't remember when exactly I saw that couple going at it in the Del Mar Plaza, whether it was before or after our phone call, but I do remember that it was one of those exquisitely lingering embraces, the sort usually followed by clothing dropping quietly to the rug. A stunning looking couple, they were standing conspicuously in the center of the walkway, so the crowds had to part to walk around them. It's an upscale three-story plaza with lots of hard-bodied Californians breezing by in designer shorts and Birkenstocks. Just about everyone floating past—it was a gorgeous late summer morning and the place was jampacked—glanced at them for an instant and then quickly looked away. I have forty-one drafts of "Kiss" on my computer, the first done in 1994 and all the rest in 1998. I must have abandoned that first draft, thinking it wasn't worth working on, and then rediscovered it four years later and decided it had potential after all. Like most of my poems, the first several drafts are laughably inept, though here and there's a phrase worth holding on to.

"Kiss" is one-tenth memory and nine-tenths confabulation. I certainly don't recall how the couple were dressed, or what they looked like, or the positions of their bodies as they embraced. Was my description of their clinch even physically possible? Could she bend the way I had her bending and still have her entire body against his? And even if that were possible, could she seem, in that position, to be stretching? I wasn't at all sure while I was writing the poem, and I'm still not sure it can be done. I moved the locale from the Enoteca del Fornaio—a wine and espresso bar in the center of the plaza—to a little coffee shop that hangs out over the Pacific Coast Highway, so that while they kissed the ocean could be in full view. For the first several drafts I had the name of the plaza wrong. The two boats with their sails that "triangulate heaven" I stole from an earlier, abandoned poem of my own. It was satisfying to make use of an image that had lain in drydock all those years. The Esmeralda is one of San Diego's good literary bookstores, and its presence there is the reason I occasionally find myself at that plaza. I never drink latté, but I like the word. On the tenth draft that "genie of steam" appears, and in the next draft the apricot scone, and with those elements that second-person implicit narrator comes into focus: a vulnerable, slightly bemused fellow offering a moment of respite from the poem's erotic center. The ocean and sailboats, the "blue cup of light," and the closing images present the expansive setting that gives the poem whatever spiritual resonance it has.

I could never decide whether that couple was "tangled" or "locked" or "coiled" in that steamy embrace; I kept going back and forth. I recall that my wife—the only person to whom I'll show my early drafts—gave me the "clutch" of dark curls well along in the process, and that seemed wonderfully right. But two sections near the end of the piece were ruinous; I was attached to them but they kept screwing everything up. One was the poem's attempt at that historic panorama, its original conception, to which I was still committed. The other problematic lines were an attempt to describe that "hubbub of jaunty boutiquers" who floated past as the couple embraced. I kept dressing and re-dressing them in an assortment of tube tops, sneakers, t-shirts and hats, but I could never get the lines to lock in, could never hear that "almost audible click" that Yeats reminds us comes when we've got it right.

Hoping it would help, I went back to the Del Mar Plaza and took another look around. I wanted to see what color the roofs of the houses were between the plaza and the ocean and what that café actually looked like. But it was mostly the feel of the place that I wanted to re-experience. The coffee shop had closed down a few months before; the area was roped off and a crew of carpenters was building counters for a brand new café. I stood by the railing looking around. I've always been partial to that strip along the Coast Highway in North County, those vivid little pastel beach towns of which Del Mar is a perfect example. There it was again: that marvelous view of the Pacific and a luminous blue sky from which came a light of such buoyant clarity that it was hard not to feel pleased—pleased at nothing in particular—to feel optimistic and refreshed.

Returning from my trip to the plaza, I found the courage to get rid of those two troublesome final sections. The boutique hunters became a single line in the middle of the poem and then, two or three drafts later, vanished altogether. Instead of trying to repair those hopelessly muddied political lines about the angel of death and how half the world is starving, I cut them loose. No doubt they'll show up again in another poem. Those troublesome lines gone, all that was left was that wonderfully generative empty space, and I was free to reinvent. The fork shining on its plate presented itself quickly, which led almost at once to the vase on the table, and then to the white tea rose, at which point the poem's final four-word sentence, which had appeared a few drafts earlier, seemed to fit perfectly. I liked that ending a good deal, though, to be honest, it felt a touch too easy, too symmetrical, too neatly epiphanic. But the more I mulled it over, the more I liked how everything led inexorably to that quietly orgasmic resolution. A taste of the eternal erotic. It is the poem's hope that the couple's pleasure will cast a glow of sensual delight over the reader, just as it had over the author. Somewhere in *The Thief's Journal,* Jean Genet writes, "I could never take lightly the idea that people were making love without me."

About the time I was finishing the poem I got a letter from Mike Carlin, asking if I had some recent work for *Mangrove,* a small Florida magazine he was editing, and advising me that he had just received a piece from a fellow in Boston that was a brazen rip-off of "Lurid Confessions," the title poem of an early collection of mine. He enclosed a copy of the poem along with the fellow's phone number. He had slightly altered most of my lines while sticking in an occasional passage of his own—the way a C-minus student-plagiarist will bollix up somebody else's text for his freshman research paper. I called the guy the next evening, introduced myself, and told him that *Mangrove* had sent me his poem. There was a long silence, and then he mumbled, "Ohhh. . .I think I can see now what must have. . .happened. . . . Well, I'll certainly withdraw it. . . . I'll withdraw it immediately. . . ." I was relieved to hear it. I didn't press him. There's always a chance a guy like that could turn out to be a screwball stalker, a nutcase with a .38. We chatted uncomfortably for a couple of minutes, both pretending it must have been an honest mistake, and finally managed to untangle ourselves enough to get off the phone.

And maybe it *was* an honest mistake. Maybe he'd jotted down my poem years before and then come upon it in an old notebook thinking it was his own. Something of the sort had once happened to Hugh MacDiarmid and it had created an international stink. Thinking about "Lurid Confessions," it dawns on me now that the second-person protagonist of that poem is the same figure who emerges as the second-person observer in "Kiss." Even the situations are much the same. For example, there's a dance in that earlier poem "with everyone making steamy love in the dark/ and you alone in a corner eating a pretzel." It could as easily have been an apricot scone. I suppose, in the end, the person we steal most shamelessly from is ourselves. I sent Mike a note thanking him for tipping me off and enclosed a copy of "Kiss" which, a couple of months later, he was kind enough to publish.

Kiss

On the patio of that little café in the Del Mar Plaza
across from the Esmeralda Bookstore, where you can
sit sipping latté & look out past the Pacific
Coast Highway onto the ocean, a couple is tangled
in one of those steamy, smoldering kisses.
His right arm coils her waist, arching her back
& drawing her toward him. He could be Sicilian,
or Lebanese, with that gorgeous complexion,
those chiseled forearms, that clutch of dark curls.
The young woman's skirt, lilac & sheer, lifts
as she stretches, levitated out of her sandals, out
of her body, her head flung back, fingers
wrapped in his curls. Her long chestnut hair
spills toward her thighs as she clings to his mouth,
to his loins, to his chest. How wickedly
beautiful both of them are! To their left,
off the North County coast, on an infinite sea,
two sailboats triangulate heaven. In the sheen
of the morning, you munch an apricot scone
& sip your cafe latté, that blue cup of light at your lips,
with its genie of steam. In its vase, on your table,
a white tea rose shimmers. Your fork
shines on its plate. Everything trembles & glows.

Pablo Neruda Would Like to
"Explain a Few Things" to You
(September 23, 2007)

It is likely that no poet of our era has been so widely read, revered, and translated as Pablo Neruda, who died on September 23, 1973, 34 years ago today. In 2003, Farrar, Straus and Giroux published a 996-page selection of Neruda's poetry translated by three-dozen American translators and edited by Ilan Stavans. Next month FSG will publish a much-abridged version under the title *I Explain a Few Things: Selected Poems* (bilingual; 355 pages, $16). Because translation is an impossible art and because Neruda is a particularly difficult poet to approximate in English, it is not altogether surprising that the translations themselves are not uniformly successful.

Given Neruda's pre-eminence, there are plenty of other versions to choose from, but almost all suffer from the same problem. In 2004, City Lights Books published *The Essential Neruda: Selected Poems*, edited by Mark Eisner (bilingual; 199 pages, $16.95). In 2005, New Directions published his Spanish Civil War poems under the title *Spain in My Heart*, translated by Donald Walsh (bilingual; 80 pages, $8). There's another useful volume of translations that Nathaniel Tarn edited for Houghton Mifflin in 1972, *Neruda: Selected Poems* (bilingual; 508 pages, $12.95). And those are only a few of the Neruda versions in English. In all these volumes, there are renditions that are splendid and others that stumble occasionally with phrases that seem awkward, unidiomatic, flat, or otherwise unconvincing.

I urge readers who want a taste of that poet's exuberant, endlessly fecund poetic genius to read the translations by Ben Belitt, originally published almost half a century ago by Grove Press and reprinted in 1994 as *Selected Poems: Pablo Neruda* (bilingual 320 pages, $15). Belitt's consistently inspired, sumptuous versions have a velocity, freshness, and authenticity that most other translators do not come close to achieving. The late Robert Creeley spoke of Ben Belitt as

Neruda's "most enduring translator," and I enthusiastically concur. Moreover, the lengthy introduction by Luis Monguió that accompanies Belitt's versions is as incisive an initiation into the poet's life and work as one is likely to find in English.

The struggle against Franco and the Spanish fascists—the heartless slaughter Neruda witnessed during Spain's civil war—galvanized his spirit and shaped him into the politically engaged "impure" poet he became. The title poem of the new selection, "I Explain a Few Things," refers to the poet's explanation of that transformation. In Belitt's sizzling version, Neruda cries out at the end:

> Turncoats
> and generals:
> . . .look well at the havoc of Spain.
> Would you know why his poems
> never mention the soil or the leaves,
> the gigantic volcanoes of the country that bore him?
> Come see the blood in the streets,
> come see
> the blood in the streets,
> come see the blood
> in the streets!

There is little doubt that Neruda's death was hastened by the U.S.-sponsored coup that overthrew the elected democracy of Salvador Allende, Neruda's friend and political ally. "We shall do all within our power to condemn Chile and all Chileans to utmost deprivation and poverty," declared U.S. Ambassador Ed Korry upon Allende's election, while Henry Kissinger explained, with Machiavellian fervor, that "The issues are much too important for the Chilean voters to be left to decide for themselves." The 17-year dictatorship of Augusto Pinochet that began on September 11th, 1973, was—however much to Washington's liking—savage and bloody for the Chilean people. Shattered by the destruction of the democracy and already gravely weakened by leukemia, Neruda died 12 days after the coup.

It would be difficult to find a poet as different from Neruda as his fellow Chilean, Nicanor Parra. A former professor of physics at the University of Santiago, Parra, who is now 93 years old, is hilariously iconoclastic and relentlessly original. *Antipoems: How to Look Better and Feel Great* (bilingual; New Directions, 130 pages, $14.95), translated by Liz Werner, assembles his poems of the past three decades. But anyone wanting to discover why Parra is so admired will have to dig up the three out-of-print collections that New Directions published decades ago: *Poems and Antipoems, Emergency Poems*, and *Antipoems: New and Selected.*

Parra's "antipoetry" eschews elaborate poetic rhetoric, opting instead for an idiom that's irreverent, comic, and as crystal-clear as good prose. In "Manifesto," translated by Miller Williams, Parra insists that

> The poets have come down from Olympus...
> We repudiate
> The poetry of dark glasses
> The poetry of the cape and sword
> The poetry of the plumed hat.

For any reader with a taste for the scathing and demotic, the best of Parra's verse is a must-read. Here is "Young Poets," this one, too, translated by Miller Williams. To my taste it's the best advice to apprentice poets ever offered:

> Write as you will
> In whatever style you like
> Too much blood has run under the bridge
> To go on believing
> That only one road is right.
> In poetry everything is permitted.
> With only this condition, of course:
> You have to improve on the blank page.

Steve Kowit translated Pablo Neruda's final book, *Incitement to Nixonicide and Praise for the Chilean Revolution.* Published in 1979 and illustrated by exiled Chilean artists, it is long out of print.

Mystique of the Difficult Poem

When I was about fifteen I fell in love with Hart Crane. The poems in *White Buildings, The Bridge,* and *Key West* shimmered with the most fragile and delicate poignancy. It was the very music of the soul's anguish. As for Crane's suicide, that was icing on the cake: it made the work even more tragic, more unbearably gorgeous. The fact that I had only the vaguest idea what he was talking about, and sometimes not even that, bothered me hardly at all until I was in my twenties and the pure music of Crane began to seem less enticing than the work of poets who, in addition to their engaging linguistic skills, actually seemed to have something coherent to say. Although Crane's pervasive obscurity was more tolerable than that of poets who were less exquisite musicians, I had by then read enough incomprehensible poetry to know that I wanted something more. I wanted marvelous music to be sure, stunning figures, an imaginative linguistic playfulness that was everywhere inspired and surprising, but I also wanted poems that spoke to me with thrilling precision and insight. The "ambiguities" that the New Critics imagined to be at the center of poetic craft seemed almost always to weaken rather than strengthen my experience of the poem. Though my first reading of a poem is likely to take pleasure in the language, the tonalities, the music and linguistic sparkle, the intelligence and taste behind the phrasing, nonetheless I find myself unlikely to finish reading a poem if it becomes apparent that the poet has no intention of communicating much of anything beyond all that language, all that music. Far be it from me to invade his privacy. If I want pure music, I can listen to Palestrina and Sam Cooke.

At about the same time as my uneasiness over modernist incoherence was growing, Allen Ginsberg, himself still a young man, was beginning to publish a poetry that was more fierce, emotionally charged, and appealingly human than anything I had read from his more staid and conventional contemporaries. And not the least of his virtues was that he was perfectly coherent. The stuff wasn't filled with footnotable literary allusions and hopelessly gnarled syntax and untrackable metaphoric acrobatics. "Howl" opened up a territory, at least for me, that the modernists had spent the first half of the century trying to close off. Suddenly the doors of possibility had been flung wide open. There was plenty of freedom, plenty of room to move around and to do what the avant garde had never dared to do—write poems in coherent English.

And then, when I was twenty-seven, I moved to the West Coast and picked up Robinson Jeffers, and was stunned anew. He was as wonderful a musician as any of the modernists I'd read, easily as fine and conscious a craftsman, but his poems, like Ginsberg's, were perfectly understandable. Jeffers' music was certainly not as ecstatic or intoxicating as Hart Crane's, but then again he never seemed ornamental, precious, histrionic; he was never without flesh and substance. Jeffers not only had something of moment to say but he managed to say it, as had Ginsberg, without resorting to a hundred subterfuges, misdirections, ambiguities. Moreover, Jeffers' vision was larger by far than that of his contemporaries, those high modernists who had dominated American poetry during the first half of the twentieth century.

Of course, in the background of my life, there had always been Whitman: larger and wiser than any poet had been before or has been since, and everywhere luminously clear. But somehow, perhaps because he was not of my century, or because he was a poet of such singular genius, his ability to speak with the utmost clarity about even the most subtle and all but inexpressible matters hadn't been able to serve me as a model. Under the influence of Whitman, Ginsberg, and Jeffers, the canonical American poets, with their inordinate love of difficulty, began to lose their luster. I became profoundly suspicious of the whole modernist enterprise. As a fledgling poet I had written enough high-flown gibberish myself to know its seductions. Though I would continue to read occasional poems and passages in poems that were thrilling, however inexplicable, the business of writing incoherent poetry seemed tiresome, and I wanted nothing to do with it.

This, I fully realize, is a minority opinion, at least among poets, academics, and critics. Though I imagine the vast bulk of the reading public feels much as I do—hence their indifference to contemporary poetry—I suspect many in the trade will find such an attitude appalling, for impenetrability is still widely admired. A recent review in *The New York Review of Books* claims, for example, as though it were a sign of the poet's talent and distinction, that Eugenio Montale "will lead commentators into all kinds of difficulty when it comes to establishing the content of many of the poems." The reviewer, discussing at length a particular twelve-line poem from Montale's early collection, *Cuttlefish,* happily admits that he has almost no idea what it means, though it is one of Montale's "simplest" lyrics. "What, overall, is the poem about?" he asks. "Even with this simplest of lyrics, the essential nub winds off into a cloud of possibilities." But this unclarity at the "essential nub" of so many Montale poems is, so the reviewer assures us, among the poet's chief virtues. The genius of Montale's work is achieved through "a prodigious density encouraging ever more complex levels of consciousness, and evoking the finest shadings of emotion colored by every variety of thought." The reviewer, Tim Parks, is a knowledgeable reader of Montale's poetry, and his praise of poetic incomprehensibility is not at all unusual among those who read poetry seriously. Nonetheless, if you look at his assertion closely, you will see that it is little more than a sophisticated version of the bemused college freshman's belief that a poem isn't really supposed to mean anything at all, so that the reader can have the pleasure of making it mean whatever he wants it to mean. When Tim Parks reminds us that "poetry in this century has become more cryptic, more private, more untranslatable," there is, in his voice, no hint of reproach. This assertion, that "difficulty" is one of modernism's defining virtues, has been so frequently injected into the body of contemporary aesthetics that it has become an unchallenged and toxic part of its bloodstream.

In *The Best American Poetry of 1990,* Jorie Graham makes perhaps the most eloquent, lengthy, and detailed recent defense of difficult and indeterminate verse. In one typical passage she writes:

When we experience a loosening of setting or point of view, and a breakdown of syntax's dependence on closure, we witness an opening up of the present-tense terrain of the poem, a privileging of delay and digression over progress. This opening up of the present moment as a terrain outside time—this foregrounding of the field of the "act of the poem"—can be explained in many ways. We might consider the way in which the idea of perfection in art seems to be called into question by many of our poets. On the one hand, some might argue today, the notion of perfection serves ultimately to make an object not so much ideal as available to a marketplace, available for ownership—something to be acquired by the act of understanding.

In this passage, Graham is recommending not just the virtues of being "indefinite" about the poem's setting, but the value of employing a syntax that guarantees that the reader will be confused about anything the poet might be trying to say. The tactical advantage of this seems to be that if readers have no idea what you're talking about and are unable to pay attention to either the narrative or the ideas (because, in fact, the poet has refused to articulate any), they will be forced to attend to "the field of the 'act of the poem,'" that is, I take it, to the manner of its saying: the phrasing, juxtapositions, music, diction, imagery, and such. This, I assume, is what she means by "an opening up of the present-tense terrain of the poem," and what she means by suggesting, in a phrase that seems somewhat inflated for its occasion, that such poems are "outside time." Apparently, if there is no narrative, no temporal instance that is being described, the poem is, therefore, "timeless." Finally, she seems to suggest that the idea of a "perfect" poem, or the attempt to write such a poem, produces something that, by virtue of being accessible to the general reader, becomes no more than a contemptible "commodity." This notion betrays a patrician haughtiness that one imagines Graham would be loath to confess more directly. Elsewhere in that essay she writes:

> The genius of syntax consists in its permitting paradoxical, "unsolvable" ideas to be explored, not merely nailed down, stored,

and owned; in its permitting the soul-forging pleasures of thinking to prevail over the acquisition of information called knowing.

For Graham, thinking and exploration seem to mean no more than being vague and ambiguous enough so that neither the author nor the reader can recognize, let alone explore, any genuine idea or perception. This, of course, is not what we tend to mean by genuine exploration of ideas but is only the façade of such exploration, and indeed what is being recommended in her essay seems nothing but a poetry of façades. Her introductory essay, made up almost entirely of this sort of piffling, goes on for some fourteen pages, all to glorify the lofty desire of the poet to resist making sense. This is the open-ended, exploratory, multi-voiced, indeterminate, opaquely textured, disjunctive, and defamiliarizing, closure-free world of postmodern poetics. And if it promotes a poetry that is "free of any user," it augurs as well a poetry that is likely to be free of many readers.

While Graham wants others to share her heady excitement over such verse, it is apt to prove a difficult sell, though her own experience of such poetry, she insists, is nothing short of redemptive. Here, in her somewhat overheated prose, she captures (or invents, depending on your view of her credibility) the rapturous, revival-meeting spirit that overcomes her when she listens to the glossolalia of incomprehensible verse:

> . . .the motion of the poem as a whole resisted my impulse to resolve it into "sense" of a rational kind. Listening to the poem, I could feel my irritable reaching after fact, my desire for resolution, graspable meaning, ownership. . . . It resisted. It compelled me to let go. The frontal, grasping motion frustrated, my intuition was forced awake. I felt myself having to "listen" with other parts of my sensibility, felt my mind being forced back down into the soil of my senses. And I saw it was the resistance of the poem—its occlusion, or difficulty—that was healing me, forcing me to privilege my heart, my intuition—parts of my sensibility infrequently called upon in my everyday experience in the marketplace of things and ideas. . . .

Mercifully less decorative is Graham's discussion, near the beginning of her essay, wherein she admits—though only, I would guess, as a rhetorical ploy—that she feels some uneasiness about the enterprise of writing poetry that resists being understood. Here, it is interesting to note, the misty cerebral romance of the rest of her essay is nowhere to be found. Here she writes in cogent English—perhaps because she has something unequivocal to say:

> Yet surely the most frequent accusation leveled against contemporary poetry is its difficulty or inaccessibility. It is accused of speaking only to itself, of becoming an irrelevant and elitist art form with a dwindling audience. . . . For how can we hear that "no one reads it," or that "no one understands it," without experiencing a failure of confidence. . . . We start believing that it is essentially anachronistic. We become anecdotal. We want to entertain. We believe we should "communicate."

In the lexicon of modernism, "anecdotal," "entertain," and "communicate" are indeed beneath contempt. They stand with "self-expression" and "sincerity" as the sort of sorry business in which only the novice and the inept engage. But if poets have far more noble goals, as Graham assures us they have, than to concern themselves with so tawdry a matter as making their poems intelligible, whatever these goals might be, they seem too ephemeral and rarified to attract the common reader, who is likely to find behind the claim little of substance and nothing of interest. Jorie Graham, one of our most praised contemporary poets, represents the aesthetic thinking of those who, like Parks, find difficulty a decided virtue. Indeed, she envisions a poetry that is not merely difficult but indeterminate, that is to say, incomprehensible. And if Graham's rationale seems a bit murky, what is one to say of something like this, the opening half-sentence of an essay by Charles Bernstein, a leading "theoretician" among the American postmodernists:

> Not "death" of the referent—rather a recharged use of the multivalent referential vectors that any word has, how words in

combination tone and modify the associations made for each of them, how "reference" then is not a one-on-one relation to an "object" but a perceptual dimension that closes in to pinpoint, nail down (this word, sputters omnitropically (the in in the which of who where what wells), refuses the buildup of image track/projection while, pointillistically, fixes a reference at each turn. . . .

More reasoned and modest than Jorie Graham's, and far less silly and dismissible than Bernstein's, is the defense of difficult poetry recently set forth by Donald Justice, who argues that certain kinds of obscurity in poetry are "not altogether destructive" ["Benign Obscurity," from *Oblivion: On Writers and Writing*, Story Line Press, 1998]. The least persuasive of his arguments is the curious notion that a poem without "hidden meanings" is likely to be trivial or frivolous, an assertion that he makes in passing and does not bother either to explain or defend. Nor does it seem likely, from anything his essay suggests, that he would be able to. Though he distinguishes a "benign" sort of obscurity from that form of obscurity for which he has less indulgence—what he characterizes as the "blanketing fog that can creep over everything"— he seems to be saving his approval, for the most part, for a poetry of magnificent music which makes the obscurity of its text seem not only palatable but perfectly appropriate, a part of the poem's necessary texture—a quality without which the poem would be something less imposing and less memorable than it is. Justice, who makes such suggestions in the most provisional and tempered language, argues that "one may be led on, and cheerfully enough at times, by precisely one's failure to grasp what is being said. And there is the excitement, meanwhile, of being in beyond one's depth." Though it is possible, I suppose, that an opaque passage or phrase in an otherwise clear text can be intriguing, and can add a certain color and excitement to a poem, I am not fully convinced of it. Though the joy of pure poetic music and language certainly has its rewards, they seem ultimately smaller rewards than such poetry would have were the same quality of language tethered to intelligible subject matter and perception. Imagine Hart Crane, for example, writing a poetry of the same verbal richness and intensity, but one that was filled with brilliant and fully lucid descriptions, narratives, characterizations, and insights. I hardly imagine it would be a lesser poetry.

Justice makes an even more interesting argument about the success of many of the more obscure poems of Hopkins, Hart Crane, and Dylan Thomas when he suggests that "the singular power of such poems seems to penetrate the emotional system directly, without ever having to pass through the understanding." But this, it seems to me, is to make too much of the fact that one can catch the flavor, subject, attitude, and emotional tone of a passage with only a few verbal cues. That certainly seems true. But with the exception of a few heady examples—poets of glorious musical skill such as the ones Justice cites—it is hard for me to think of many poets who can carry the day on their musicianship alone. It is to suggest, I think, that the content of poems really is an unimportant aspect. Perhaps that is true for Justice. I know it is not true for me. His third argument is that the obscurity of a narrative poem such as E. A. Robinson's "Eros Turanos" might, perhaps, be "expressive of the very understanding the poem is intended to carry." By this he seems to mean that the poem's narrative lack of clarity might be rooted in—that is, it might be a consciously formal or strategic correlative for—the moral complexity of the situation it purports to describe. I confess at once that the suggestion seems farfetched, and the very fact that Justice himself is so uneasy about postulating it leads me to believe he's about as unconvinced by it as I am. I suspect, rather, that he so much admires both those parts of the Robinson poem that are clear and the prosodic and writerly skill of the whole that he has allowed his good common sense to be swayed by a number of other critics who admire the poem, in part, for the very reason that it doesn't entirely make sense. To my taste, Robinson's best poems are, however subtle in their narrative strategies, nonetheless perfectly clear. When he fails, which is often enough, it is because of an inability or unwillingness to tell his story with sufficient clarity. "Eros Turanos" has fine passages and, here and there, admirable moments of complex psychological portraiture but, in the end, the poem collapses beneath the weight of its unclarity. Although Justice wonders if those critics might be right that its very unclarity is a virtue, he seems uneasy about the proposition and not entirely convinced, and his essay ends with the most modest of claims. For certain poems or certain kinds of poems, a degree of obscurity, he posits, is simply unavoidable, and with such poems "the obscurity is no handicap, perhaps even has its uses—can we claim this much?"

It seems to me that the widespread critical belief that poetry needn't communicate has had disastrous consequences for the art, and that a shockingly large part of the poetry of our own time is, with its blanketing fog of obscurity, altogether unreadable. In the end, neither avant-garde Language Poets like Charles Bernstein nor well-meaning postmodernists like Jorie Graham are to be blamed for this mess. Children of the age of theory, the postmodernists argue that communication isn't really possible anyhow and that no reading of a "text" can be "privileged" over any other: that is to say, language itself is indeterminate. But this idea is by no means the radical break with the modernist tradition that it might at first seem. It is, rather, its natural extension: postmodernist "indeterminacy" being the logical extension—or at least the *reductio ad absurdum*—of the defining modernist penchant for difficulty. It wasn't Charles Bernstein, after all, but T. S. Eliot who suggested that "meaning" was a questionable expedient that we could well do without, nothing more than meat thrown to the watchdogs while the burglar robbed the house. It need be said at once that Eliot never practiced quite so radical a poetics as his remark suggests. At its best, which is a good deal of the time, his poetry, however nonlinear, is brilliantly coherent. Though the various settings of a poem like "Prufrock" continue to shift disconcertingly, in Eliot's controlled hands the collaged, unanchorable narrative, a fusion of interior anxieties and exterior perceptions and assertions, remains, however complex and novel, brilliantly intelligible.

By the Forties, the fashion for the difficult had become so pervasive that the subject of incoherence and indeterminacy rarely arose as a significant issue in critical discourse. And although a good number of our best poets are no longer engaged in that sort of enterprise, and take pleasure in writing a poetry that, however wild, subtle, and surprising, is perfectly lucid, indecipherability is still much in vogue, as one can prove by glancing through just about any contemporary anthology or poetry journal. This opacity, which has effectively killed off any possibility of a large American readership, has been a reigning fashion in conventional poetry for almost a century now, and while it is still common to hear the virtues of difficulty extolled in the critical literature, it is exceedingly rare to find even the most tepid dissent. If there are serious poets and critics who are appalled by this facet of the contemporary aesthetic, they have been politic enough to keep their mouths shut. But its absence from serious consideration is probably less a matter of conscious decision than the fact that the ideology is so pervasive it has become an all but unchallengeable assumption, as if difficulty were a necessary function of what poetry is, a fundamental condition of the art itself.

Which is why, I suppose, the issue has not been a significant feature of any of the poetry pie fights of the past few decades. Fought out at the edges of the Great American Kulturkampf—that low-intensity protracted warfare between an ascendant conservatism and a liberalism that dare not speak its name—these periodic skirmishes, often emblematic of the larger national conflict being waged over America's soul, reveal a good deal about who we are and what we believe. A few years back, for example, Joseph Epstein, in a bit of conservative nostalgia, provoked an amusing squabble by suggesting that our verse had notably degenerated since the era of Eliot and Stevens. Another battle raged over the "neo-formalists," who wish to return us to the prosodic rigors of the past. At the same time, there was the marginally memorable flap over the deconstructionist aesthetic of the Language Poets who were either registering a monumental epistemic breakthrough, as they themselves loudly proclaimed, or were merely "long on theory," as Allen Ginsberg once pointedly suggested. Apparently, many mainstream poets who smirk at the relentless incoherence of those avant-gardists delude themselves with the comforting notion that their own brand of highly complex, disjunctive, and imagistically dense poetry is, if one only reads sensitively enough, perfectly intelligible. In the latest poetry brouhaha, Harold Bloom, a tireless advocate of difficulty in poetry, has registered his pique at the new multicultural barbarism that is undermining the Western intellectual tradition. With the universities' urgency to teach an inclusive, gender-conscious, multi-ethnic curriculum, it is Bloom's fear that the "major" poets and novelists of the English tradition will be abandoned by the academy in favor of undistinguished figures whose only virtue is that they are representatives of various "under-represented" minorities. At the same time, so Bloom would have it, the critical establishment has been seriously undermined by post-structuralist, and decidedly anti-canonical, notions of literature, language, and culture. American poetry is self-destructing, he insists, under the influence of "the French diseases, the mock-feminists, the commissars, the gender-and-power freaks, the hosts of new historicists and old materialists."

In his essay, which appears as his introduction to *The Best of the Best American Poetry: 1988-1997* (a later volume of the same series in which Jorie Graham's essay appeared), Bloom is indignant at the dumbing-down of the university curriculum as indicated by the widespread sanctioning of cultural studies departments: that is to say, all those Black, Hispanic, Feminist, and Queer *arrivistes* who have managed to elbow their way into seats at the academic banquet. More particularly, he is in a dither over the likes of Lady Mary Chudleigh and Anne Killigrew having insinuated themselves into those hernia-inducing tomes that undergraduates are forced to lug from building to building on Tuesdays and Thursdays. This reprehensible attack on the Western canon, he assures us, is a byproduct of "cultural guilt" and successful hectoring by "The School of Resentment."

Apparently, in tilting toward affirmative action set-asides—toward homosexuals, women, undeserving poets of color, the politically correct and hyphenated-Americans—these offending anthologies have been insidiously undermining the foundations of our civilization. Not surprisingly, in the many rejoinders that have been made to his broadside—most notably in the Spring '98 *Boston Review,* which was devoted to such responses—he is roundly attacked by a number of poets for his cultural conservatism and, by a few postmodernists, for his aesthetic conservatism. Carol Muske, in the brightest and most eloquent of those published responses, defends the revisionist Heath and the revised Norton by recalling, during her college days, paging through anthologies of poetry, in vain, looking for the names of women. Surely there was some other female writer besides Dickinson or Sappho? Maybe the Countess of Pembroke? How thrilling it was, back then, to find a female name, even if it was attached to a relatively uninspiring poem. It was thrilling just to see that women wrote, were published. So, room had to be made for these other voices—beyond the best. And beyond The Best of.

Several of the other *Boston Review* respondents take Bloom to task for one or another of his blind spots. But it seems to me both significant and lamentable that not a single essayist responding to Bloom took issue with what I take to be his most pernicious assertion: "Authentic American poetry," he declares in that bilious introduction, is necessarily difficult. . .our situation needs aesthetic and cognitive difficulty. . .it is our elitist art, though that elite has nothing to do with social class, gender, erotic preference, ethnic strain, race, or sect. "We live in the mind," Stevens said.

This insistence on poetic opacity is questioned only by those postmodernists among the *Boston Review* respondents who insist that poetry ought to be more incomprehensible yet. Apparently what Bloom finds objectionable among the deconstructionist critics, those pernicious purveyors of "the French diseases," is their subversively anti-hierarchic beliefs about literature and culture, and has nothing to do with the macaronic density of their language. This is hardly surprising: the love of jargon-saturated, dizzyingly complex rhetorical footwork which those infected with the "French diseases" find so attractive is not, after all, so different from the kind of academic flapdoodle upon which his own critical reputation rests.

As for his insistence on the very necessity for difficulty, Bloom is in the absurd position of having to claim that even Walt Whitman was, "above all else, a very difficult poet," while asserting with a straight face that Wallace Stevens, T. S. Eliot, and John Ashbery are Whitman's true heirs. In order to spin Whitman in the image of poets so utterly inimical to his spirit, he simply stands Whitman on his head. On an earlier occasion he had declared that Whitman's statement of ecstatic longing, "To touch my person to some one else's is about as much as I can stand," was the poet's confession that he found human touch repulsive. An unreconstructed Freudian, Bloom is capable of making any statement mean what he wishes it to mean. Freud's main technique for this kind of convenient fast shuffle was "reaction formation," a putative psychic mechanism that transformed things into their opposites. When a patient said or dreamed something that confounded the analyst's interpretation, it was simply a reaction formation: that is, the patient's meaning was the very opposite of what it seemed to be. Thus, according to Bloom, "Whitman's poetry generally does the opposite of what he proclaims its work to be: it is reclusive, evasive, hermetic, nuanced, and more onanistic even than homoerotic." This, of course, is embarrassing nonsense. As for living in one's head, a la Wallace Stevens, that is precisely what Whitman is at pains to warn us against. When he tells us that he is "Both in and out of the game, and watching and wondering at it"—a line Bloom quotes in his essay—it is not, as that critic assumes, to register the kind of self-conscious alienation from life that his favorite modernists display. Rather, the poet is declaring that he does not live in thrall to the common delusions of the ego, but has awakened into the unmediated world: that he is not an intellect filled with attitudes and opinions, but an empty, observing awareness. As for "difficulty," Whitman proclaims: "I will not have in my writing any elegance or effect or originality to hang in the way between me and the rest like curtains. I will have nothing hang in the way, not the richest curtains." Against the corollary modernist principle that poems are made of words, not ideas, he memorably declares: "The words of my poem nothing, the drift of it everything." But the case of Whitman also offers to us the cautionary example of the dangers of canonical literary judgments: Our "best" poets and critics, blind to his genius, dismissed him as a vulgar eccentric, until the zeitgeist shifted in mid-century and everyone suddenly noticed his bearded figure towering above our literature.

However, the most curious and provocative portion of Bloom's essay was not his attack on multiculturalism or his absurd revision of Whitman, but his attack on Adrienne Rich, whose *Best American Poetry of 1996* was the only one of David Lehman's annual series from which Bloom did not draw work for his *Best of the Best*. Rich's anthology is emblematic for Bloom of the wretched state of literary affairs, exemplifying everything that's wrong with the new affirmative action poetics. It is of a badness not to be believed, because it follows the criteria now operative: what matters most are the race, gender, sexual orientation, ethnic origin, and political purpose of the would-be poet. I ardently wish I were being hyperbolical, but in fact I am exercising restraint. . . . Bursting with sincerity, the 1996 volume is a Stuffed Owl of bad verse, and of much badness that is neither verse nor prose.

With this judgment at least three of the *Boston Review* respondents unequivocally concur: one, J.D. McClatchy, is an enthusiastic advocate of difficult poetry. The other two, Marjorie Perloff and Reginald Shepherd, disdain meaning altogether. Perloff finds many of Rich's choices "relentlessly PC. . .maudlin, self-righteous, boring, and ultimately just plain incompetent." A tireless champion of the poetry of impenetrability, it is hardly surprising that she would find Rich's penchant for the accessible, emotional, and socially engaged antithetical to her tastes. For Perloff, any poetry that doesn't exhibit an uncompromising indeterminacy smacks of the platitudinous and sentimental: soap opera masquerading as art. Not surprisingly, Perloff faults Bloom, too, for his reactionary poetic tastes, his inability to appreciate the "genuinely radical poetry now being written," by which she means the unabashedly incomprehensible writers whom she has been championing for the past many years. McClatchy's criticism, less idiosyncratic than Perloff's, is more telling for the fact that it shares Bloom's particular elitist predilections. The first poem in Rich's volume, written by a prisoner at the Pelican Bay State Prison serving a twenty-two-year sentence for burglary, is, he declares, a piece of "utter banality" and symptomatic of her volume as a whole. With its "clutter of clichés, sentimentality, confused syntax, and flailing gestures," it is a poem that McClatchy finds downright campy. An attempt to express the dehumanizing horror of a prison notorious for its systemic brutality, "In the Tombs," by Latif Asad Abdullah, is indeed an unsuccessful poem, but not because of sentimentality or platitudes. Rather, its flaw is a more common one: the inability to make its case with the incisive power that its subject demands. On the other hand, McClatchy's use of the word "campy" to characterize a poem about such enormous personal anguish strikes me as rather chilling, and perfectly typical of the crippling emotional disability that he shares with many of his fellow academic poets and literary critics. For such writers any unarmored feeling is to be avoided at all cost, a need that is likely to make the distancing strategies of obliqueness and opacity seem appealing. Given that pathology, one understands why to such writers "sincerity"—a word that both McClatchy and Bloom use as a smirking pejorative—would seem threatening. Actually, Abdullah's poem about Pelican State—one of the collection's few unpolished pieces—is not at all symptomatic of the Adrienne Rich anthology, while the weaknesses of Bloom's book can, I believe, be fairly characterized by McClatchy's own lengthy contribution to that collection. Like one of those wits who imagines himself endlessly amusing, McClatchy's poem, "An Essay on Friendship," rambles on for some two hundred and seventy lines in that excruciatingly sophisticated, three-martini tone peculiar to the academic gentility. More ruinously, the poem's narrative thread is willfully obscure. McClatchy, who is by no means an untalented writer, and whose poems, though sometimes uninteresting are almost always skillfully composed, tells us in his little explanatory note at the end of the volume that certain sections of "An Essay on Friendship" will only be understood by readers familiar with Renoir's film, *Rules of the Game.* Clearly, then, the poet has only the most minimal interest in communicating much of anything with his reader: whether or not he is understood is of little concern to him. Not far from McClatchy's endnote in the Bloom anthology is another telling one, in which Richard Wilbur wryly reports that after his wife had read his poem "Lying," she remarked, "well, you've finally done it; you've managed to write a poem that's incomprehensible from beginning to end." But immediately Wilbur assures us that on second reading she found it "quite forthright" (no doubt with a little cueing), and then tells us that he makes no apology for the fact that the poem requires several readings. "Provided it's any good, a poem which took months to write deserves an ungrudging quarter hour from the reader." But Wilbur's scolding the reader for not spending enough time puzzling out his poem misses the point. One is reminded of Norman Mailer's apology, some decades back, for having used as an epigraph to one of his early collections of essays the admonition: "Do not understand me too quickly." Older and wiser, Mailer had come to understand that if even experienced readers were misapprehending him, the fault was his own: clarity is the writer's responsibility, not the reader's. Surely when Richard Wilbur's poems are a joy to read, as they so often are, it is because that exquisitely deft versification is the brilliant vehicle for ideas and arguments rendered with lapidary clarity. Here, for example, are the final stanzas of that wonderful "Aubade," in which he argues to his beloved that staying in bed is the most reasonable of her options:

> Think of all the time you are not
> Wasting, and would not care to waste,
> Such things, thank God, not being to your taste.
> Think what a lot
> Of time, by woman's reckoning,
> You've saved, and so may spend on this,
> You who had rather lie in bed and kiss
> Than anything.
> It's almost noon you say? If so,
> Time flies, and I need not rehearse
> The rosebud-theme of centuries of verse.
> If you must go,
> Wait for a while, then slip downstairs
> And bring us up some chilled white wine,
> And some blue cheese, and crackers, and some fine
> Ruddy-skinned pears.

Though he believes adamantly that "strong poetry is always difficult," it is noteworthy that Harold Bloom includes in *The Best of the Best* a good number of poems that are perfectly clear, and these are the poems that are most likely to raise the hair on the back of one's neck: poems by May Swenson, Kay Ryan, Amy Clampitt, Allen Ginsberg, Ed Hirsch, Philip Levine, and Molly Peacock, among others. Donald Justice is represented with a memorable elegy for Henri Coulette in which the poet asks his friend to "Come back and help me with these verses/

Whisper to me some beautiful secret that you remember from life."
Although Donald Hall has a strained exercise in vatic rage, an ersatz-
Ginsbergian rant that strikes a note decidedly false, it is followed by
one of his exemplary poems, this one about Jane Kenyon's dying, a
poem that is the very model of simplicity, clarity, and unadorned
honesty. The two poems together make a fine study in the dangers of
the postured and the virtues of the sincere, the authentically felt. Also
of note are two stunningly powerful and perfectly accessible pieces by
Louise Glück. In "Vespers," the narrator argues with God for having let
her tomatoes die:

> . . .I doubt
> you have a heart, in our understanding of
> that term. You who do not discriminate
> between the dead and the living, who are, in
> consequence,
> immune to foreshadowing, you may not know
> how much terror we bear, the spotted leaf,
> the red leaves of the maple falling
> even in August, in early darkness: I am
> responsible
> for these vines.

All told, Rich's anthology is just about as good as Bloom's, its major
virtue being that she has a lively eye for the coherent and the
unashamedly human, the openly emotional and exuberant kind of
engaged poetry that many American poets have been writing since the
'60s. Were there anthologies filled exclusively with the work of such
writers, American poetry would have a fighting chance of regaining its
rightful audience. Rich assuredly does not agree with Bloom that the
aesthetic is an autonomous realm independent of political and cultural
ideologies, or that poetry is ruined by social engagement, or that a less
rarified, intellectualized poetic is the death blow to our literary
culture. Not surprisingly, there is a good deal less here of the
mannered rhetoric that pervades Bloom's choices and a good deal
more of a poetry awake to the world outside of the poet's head. Since a
good two-thirds of Rich's offerings are by well-known, well-respected

poets, and since her volume contains, as he grudgingly acknowledges, the work of several of the same writers that appear in his own, Bloom's claim against it is seriously undermined. Surely it was not discerning taste but sheer petulance that kept him from being able to acknowledge how many fine poems she has brought together in her collection. He might not have been able to appreciate the emotional power of Raymond Patterson's "Harlem Suite" or Luis Alberto Urrea's long, rhapsodic, open-hearted elegy for his father, not because he harbors any racism—he most likely does not—but because that sort of gritty, heart-centered, anti-intellectualized poetry, which owes nothing to the tradition of Wallace Stevens, is the sort for which he has little patience. Though Bloom's abhorrence of explicit social compassion might have made him immune to the powerful, history-drenched poems of Alicia Ostriker and Wang Ping, and to the fine, socially engaged ones of Ann Winters, Chase Twitchell, Gary Soto, and Alma Villanueva—for compassion, like sincerity and accessibility, is not a modernist virtue—there are several pieces in her anthology that would undoubtedly have interested him had he not been in such high dudgeon. He would likely have been drawn to W. S. Merwin's "Lament for the Makers," with its nicely jagged, Dunbar-esque rhythms and off-rhymed couplets, especially given its generous sprinkling of literary gossip, and it is hard to believe he wouldn't have given serious consideration to "Touch Me," a Stanley Kunitz love poem that is surely going to find its way into numerous anthologies of twentieth-century verse. Both poems share the traditional metrical skills that Bloom, for all his admiration for Ashbery, most admires. Rich's anthology also contains finely made pieces by Reynolds Price, Jane Kenyon, Naomi Shihab Nye, Yusef Komunyakaa, and half a dozen others that would certainly have merited his attention. She is to be congratulated for looking beyond the rhetorical commonplaces of conventional poetry and including pieces that are far removed from the academic mainstream. Not the least of the poems she chose for her anthology is a sestina by Katherine Alice Power, an antiwar radical who is presently serving an eight-to-twelve-year sentence for participating in a bank robbery back in 1970 which ended in the murder of a policeman. Her surrender in 1993 provoked enormous national publicity and debate. Power's impressive and touching sestina for her son is a useful example of how to employ a form that even in the hands of competent poets tends to sound forced, formulaic, and insincere. On the other hand, the clunkers in the Rich anthology share with Bloom's clunkers the same overriding flaw: they're incomprehensible. And by this I do not mean to suggest that clarity determines the quality of poetry: most emphatically it does not. Surely much of the most hilariously inept and amateurish verse being written is perfectly intelligible. What I am asserting is that although clarity is by no means a sufficient condition for successful poetry, it is, in all but the rarest of cases, a necessary one. And yet for certain poets and critics of our time, as I have been at pains to point out, obscurity is an overriding virtue. What kind of poetry is it, then, that they want? What might it look and sound like? In the texts I have been examining, the most explicit answer to that question comes from Reginald Shepherd, the third *Boston Review* correspondent who, implicitly at least, can find little merit in a poetry that is coherently engaged in the world beyond language. Shepherd, like Marjorie Perloff, rejects any poetry that makes so much as a grain of sense, for such poetry, according to him, refuses to "honor language," something that is done, apparently, by treating it as an end in itself. Shepherd wants a poetry of "strangeness and opacity," one that exhibits a "resistance to communication. . .which restores language to itself," criteria with which Perloff would surely agree.

Understandably, Shepherd is reticent to attack Adrienne Rich's anthology because it contains one of his own poems, so his example of what poetry should not be is drawn instead from Bloom's *Best of the Best.* He faults Bloom for canonizing Amy Clampitt, whom he characterizes as an erudite and amiable writer, but one "for whom language has no independent existence: she has something of greater or lesser interest to 'say' and she says it more or less well. But poetry is not versified thought. . .nor is it amiable or well mannered." In reiterating the aesthetic stance of the Language Poets, it seems curiously off-point for Shepherd to single out Amy Clampitt rather than a less exuberant poet. Surely one hopes there was a reason for his choice beyond the cute pun on her name, just the sort of sophomoric "word-play" that postmodernists are often unembarrassedly given to. But Shepherd could not have chosen a more inappropriate example, for there are few contemporaries who seemed as utterly in love with the succulence of words, the intoxicating pleasures of language. If anyone of our era ought by rights to have been characterized as a poet who was language-centered, it is surely Amy Clampitt, a poet who manages to be wildly intoxicating with her language while remaining perfectly intelligible. This is how "My Cousin Muriel," a poem about her dying cousin that Bloom wisely chose to use for *The Best of the Best,* begins:

> From Manhattan, a glittering shambles
> of enthrallments and futilities, of leapers
> in leotards, scissoring vortices blurred,
> this spring evening, by the *punto in aria*
> of hybrid pear trees in bloom (no troublesome
> fruit to follow) my own eyes are drawn to—
> childless spinner of metaphor, in touch
> by way of switchboard and satellite, for
> the last time ever, with my cousin Muriel. . .

But this sort of delicious and truly language-centered writing makes far too much sense for Reginald Shepherd, who tells us in his essay that poetry ought to be an escape from meaning. Shepherd concludes his brief essay with four lines from a contemporary poem that he admires "because something is happening in them that happens nowhere else." This is his exemplary excerpt:

> Vagrant, back, my scrutinies
> The candid deformations as with use
> A coat or trousers of one dead
> Or as habit smacks of certitude.

In the presence of such writing it is difficult to know what to say. Surely in the prison house of language, poets writing in this manner have opted for solitary confinement. If one is going to "escape from meaning" and foreground other qualities, one would imagine that either music, striking linguistic and figurative invention, or deft and original phrasing would be evident. If one is going to be excruciatingly difficult or downright incomprehensible, we need in compensation other virtues. One needs, at the very least, the intensity and profound musical and linguistic skill of authentic poetic composition. One thinks of the evocative, heartbreaking music of Hart Crane, or the coryambic and often rigorously measured verse of Dylan Thomas, or the syntactically wrenched and passionate strangeness of Vallejo, or the hypnogogic dream-swirling Dionysian difficulties of Hopkins or Berryman or Rimbaud or Cesaire, or of Robert Lowell's early work with its headlong velocity and gorgeously gnarled intensities, or of the strange, disquieting magic we encounter in someone like Antonin Artaud, for whom surrealism was not so much a novel technique as a desperate means of plumbing his tormented depths. "Resistance to communication," the passage Reginald Shepherd has quoted, certainly exhibits. But flattened of affect and bereft of music, this kind of silliness doesn't even have the virtue, any longer, of novelty. That such lines restore language to itself seems questionable—to put it mildly. Given that the defining property of language is communicability, shouldn't this sort of thing be called "Anti-Language Poetry"?

Although poetry often attempts to transcend the limits of language, in an attempt to invent such an idiom legions of twentieth-century poets have mistaken mystification for mystery. The real mystery of poetry is that it inexplicably opens the reader to that which is all but inexpressible. It is as though one had used a ladder to climb onto a roof with a spectacular view and then discovered that the ladder upon which one had climbed does not, in fact, exist—to use Ludwig Wittgenstein's provocative metaphor. But mystification, whether of the modernist or post-structuralist variety, is simply the pretense of having climbed anywhere. Poetry, when it is at its most ineffable, transports us to places we had no reason to believe language could take us. What is needed for this task is the most luminous vision, the most receptive spirit, and the most crystalline possible clarity of presentation. Our period's infatuation with the opaque has been, in the end, a seriously misdirected effort. The most eloquent response to that wrong turning was made by Robinson Jeffers more than seventy years ago, when the modernist agenda had hardly begun and long before its eccentric notions had come to dominate aesthetic discourse. Prescient as ever, Jeffers wrote in the introduction to his 1938 Random House *Selected Poetry:*

> Long ago, before anything included here was written, it became evident to me that poetry—if it was to survive at all—must reclaim some of the power and reality that it was so hastily surrendering to prose. The modern French poetry of that time, and the most "modern" of the English poetry, seemed to me thoroughly defeatist, as if poetry were in terror of prose, and desperately trying to save its soul from the victor by giving up its body. It was becoming slight and fantastic, abstract, unreal, eccentric; and was not even saving its soul, for these are generally anti-poetic qualities. It must reclaim substance and sense, and physical and psychological reality. . . . Another formative principle came to me from a phrase of Nietzsche's: "The poets? The poets lie too much." I was nineteen when the phrase stuck in my mind; a dozen years passed before it worked effectively, and I decided not to tell lies in verse. Not to feign any emotion that I did not feel; not to pretend to believe in optimism or pessimism, or irreversible progress, not to say anything because it was popular, or generally accepted, or fashionable in intellectual circles, unless I myself believed it; and not to believe easily. These negatives limit the field; I am not recommending them but for my own occasions.

Let us, by all means, have a poetry of the most incandescent verbal pyrotechnics, of the most restlessly experimental and original design. Let us have poems that astonish the reader at every turn. Let our poets attend to making it new with nearly as much fervor as they attend to making it true. But on those occasions when we fail to communicate, let us no longer imagine we have succeeded at something larger and grander. Let us not blame our failures on the intellectual poverty of our readers, or on their inability to register complex ambiguities, or on their irritable reaching after fact, or on the ineptitude of their teachers, or on the seductions of the media, or on crass materialism, or on the philistine vulgarity of our culture, or on—well, whatever else seems convenient to blame for our own failures. Let us no longer be gulled into imagining that rhetorical sophistication and verbal panache in the absence of genuine, communicated perception can create a poetry that is genuinely complex, textured, multilayered, exploratory, intuitive, and profoundly insightful, a poetry worth careful study. They create, rather, poems that are hardly worth reading through once. Harold Bloom notwithstanding, our situation demands aesthetic and cognitive clarity.

"They have the numbers, we the heights" is the heroic epigraph Bloom uses for his dyspeptic rant against those who would open the doors of what he calls our "elitist art" and let in some air. They are words attributed by Thucydides to the Spartan commander at Thermopylae. No doubt Bloom, our self-appointed Keeper of the Canon, imagines himself the heroic captain of the last small band of stalwart Western aesthetes, holding the gates of the Temple of Art against the raucous assaults of the parti-colored resenters, the Great Unwashed. But the very mean-spiritedness of his attack belies the pretense that he represents some nobler and higher ground. The only heights that the defenders of the aesthetic of difficulty have to offer us are the heights of arrogance, exclusivity, and self-aggrandizement, and the only effect of composing one's poetry from such heights is to insure that it remains chilly, windy, and unlikely to be heard.

Theology

That Salome,
she sure could dance.

—from *The First Noble Truth*, by Steve Kowit

The 97,000-Mile-a-Minute Poetry Machine

It was in Stanley Kunitz's YMHA poetry workshop in the early '60s that my friend Jack Marshall and I met the young poet Kathy Fraser. She was a stunning young voluptuary with flaming red hair and country-milk flesh. A knockout. She was a junior editor at *Mademoiselle* and dressed the part. Still somewhat star-struck by New York, she gave the appearance of a wide-eyed farm-girl from the heartland tho in fact she was a good deal cannier than she let on. The daughter of a Presbyterian minister, she hid her feisty spirit behind the saccharin façade demanded of a small-town minister's daughter. Kathy had an enthusiasm for poetry equal to Jack's, but, far more convivial, she had a more sophisticated and ambitious eye for the New York culture scene. By mid-semester they had discovered each other. They sizzled around more or less incommunicado for several months and then surfaced, still breathing heavily and somewhat gleefully embarrassed, at Kathy's place on the Lower East Side.

Now and again I'd subway down to see them, but it was awkward and I was clearly something of an intruder. Jack and I would go out for one of our long walks—the kind we used to take in the old days around Sheepshead Bay. Kathy didn't entirely approve of me, and I have no doubt that had I been a female friend she would have gladly ripped my face off for looking at Jack admiringly. Beside which, she heartily disapproved my affection for marijuana. She was terrified that I was going to turn Jack into one of those degraded addicts holding up liquor stores and nodding out in back alleys in the reefer-madness mode of movies made to terrify high school students in the Midwest.

On the other hand, given the impressive number of acid freaks who eventually flew out windows, junkies who O.D.'d in their bathtubs, the legion who in the decade to come were to burn themselves out behind a chemical bliss of one stripe or another, Kathy's instincts weren't so far off the mark. Be that as it may, there was a decided tension between us and I came around less and less frequently. But on several of those occasions when I did hazard a visit, they mentioned with a good deal of enthusiasm the poetry readings at the *10th Street Coffee House*. One evening when I had nothing better to do—the Thalia movie house up where I was living was probably running something I'd already seen twice—I decided to check the place out. It was a cozy little hideaway, clean and well-kept, with a dozen mahogany tables and a counter with an espresso machine: probably the only coffee house in the city without bullfight posters on the walls. An open reading was under way, a fellow named C.V.J. Anderson presiding. I put my name on the waiting list, sat down, and ordered a hot chocolate. A dozen or so people were sitting around the room waiting for their turn at the stage, mostly scurvy looking kids in their twenties, like me. A sorrier collection of neophyte poets would be hard to imagine. They whispered their poems with a nervous, solipsistic intensity, or declaimed them with shrill bravado, or managed to do a little of both. Verses full of distant faerie realms and coal-dark abysses of the soul. The sort of hyperventilated, angst-ridden verse one would expect. I don't remember what I read when my turn came but I don't imagine it was very much better.

When the reading was over, C.V.J. came over and introduced himself. Chester was a fast-talking baby-faced veteran of the American poetry underground with a kind of breathless hysteria indigenous to speed-freaks and chain-smokers. There was a seductive lilt to his voice that permeated not only his conversation and his poetry, but the way he moved. He was of that feline breed that bounces up and down on the balls of his feet, his heels never quite touching the ground. With his rapid-fire delivery, you always had the impression that Chester had just said something particularly witty that you hadn't quite understood. I'd generally catch the drift but rarely the details. He let it be known that he had some kind of rare disease and had been assured that he had no more than seven years to live. He was a good writer and a fine musician, something of a virtuoso on the soprano recorder. I heard him play some Bach once in his cavernous apartment and it was an impressive affair. Among the tasks he had planned for those last seven years of his life was whipping an international baroque chamber group into shape. The other plan, as I recall, was winning the Pulitzer.

After I'd been reading at the *10th Street* for a couple of months, Chester and Mickey Ruskin, the owner, decided that it was time for me to do a solo reading. It was the first one I'd ever done and I remember almost nothing about it except that Bob Kelly, that enormous globe of a poet, sat in the front row walking a book of paper matches from knuckle to knuckle of his right hand—to let everyone know he was bored to distraction. No doubt with good reason. Mickey paid me ten bucks for the reading and treated my girlfriend Rozzie and me to a meal. Everyone knew Mickey later when he owned *Les Deux Megots, The Ninth Circle,* and *Max's Kansas City,* but back then he was just getting started—a skinny, soft-spoken chap with a law degree, a fondness for poets and artists, and a quiet, good-natured civility. In those days Diane Wakoski was Poetry Queen of *The Tenth Street.* Hardly yet published and certainly not known beyond the circle of young New York poets, she already had a devoted underground following. It was clear to everyone that she was a real talent—obsessive, idiosyncratic, and totally committed. An original. In those early days, Diane was of the school of disassociative surrealism—that great leap backwards in American poetry—a bit of Stevens and a bit of Apollinaire—her poems full of magenta hats and erotic avocado pits. She wrote long, epiphanic dream-epics and symbolist psychodramas and seemed to have at least one new powerhouse of a poem every week. Her stuff never failed to bring down the house.

One evening Diane showed up for the open reading accompanied by a large and rather peculiar-looking entourage of people in funny hats, all of whom had the aura of being folks one ought to know. About the only one I vaguely recognized was her boyfriend LaMonte Young, a fallen-away classical pianist who'd become a hermetic composer of the most mystical and minimalist stripe. I'd recently caught a concert of his at a downtown loft which consisted of one note played at two and a half-minute intervals. The piece was followed by the work of a beautiful Japanese dada composer named Yoko Ono. That one, as I recall, consisted of two notes on the flute. LaMonte Young was dressed heroically in a maroon cape. As I recall, both Julian Beck and Judith Malina were there too, but I didn't recognize them. Among the others in her party was Jackson Mac Low, a poet few of us had heard of. A small, neatly-dressed, somber-looking fellow, he reminded me of certain heavy-souled rabbinical students I'd had the misfortune of knowing in my student days. When his turn came, Mac Low read an interminable piece that seemed utterly disembodied and pointless— even more pointless than the earnest poetry of the ordinary avant-garde. Not so much *utterly* as *emphatically* pointless. The pointlessness seemed, if anything, to be the point.

The house rules were that every poet had five minutes—since there was always a pack of hungry geniuses waiting in the wings. After Mac Low had been up there a good fifteen minutes and the poem, if that's what it was, showed no signs of winding toward a conclusion—or toward anything at all for that matter, a wave of grumbling spread through the audience. It was only a matter of minutes before somebody whistled. Right on its heels were a couple of catcalls and Bronx cheers. I don't remember who it was, but somebody jumped out of his seat to tell Mac Low to get the fuck off the stage before he kicked his lights out. Though there wasn't any verbal assent to the proposition, there weren't any protests either. Mac Low, finishing up quickly, picked up his manuscript and returned to his table in a dignified huff. A minute later, after a quick huddle, Jackson, Diane, LaMonte, and the rest of their party of underground celebrities paraded out of the place looking neither right nor left—all grandly offended. It was a notable exit and—as it turned out—a watershed event in the subterranean history of American avant-garde poetry.

The moment they were out the door the screaming began. Though a lot of us felt we'd had every right to give him the hook, still and all we'd offended a lot of star attractions. A short-story writer named Hank Bauer—an old friend of Jack Marshall's—made a lengthy speech to the effect that life on the planet Earth was undeservedly and brutally short and by his calculation we had lost a good twenty-seven minutes of our irrecoverable orgone energy listening to that insufferable and idiotic crap. He proposed that we pass a resolution barring the fellow from ever being permitted back into *Les Deux Megots* on any pretext, even to use the bathroom, and went so far as to suggest a public petition barring him from all Lower East Side and Greenwich Village coffee houses that held or were contemplating at some time in the future the possibility of holding poetry readings.

At this point Howard Ant stepped to the front of the assembled poets and guided the clamjamfry in an altogether different direction. Howard was a good friend of Diane's and told us forthrightly that he thought we'd been boorish in the extreme and that we had every reason to be ashamed of what had just occurred. Our clear obligation was to invite the fellow back with our apologies and ask him to do a solo reading for us—perhaps as soon as the following week. Howard's Harvard Law School training in rhetoric, argumentation, and dignified cajolery and coercion, plus the fact that everyone liked and respected him—he was a man of good heart and good common sense—ended up winning the day. There were a few boos and go-fuck-your-mothers— but in the end the group was agreeable to the idea. Yes, let's by all means have the fellow back to give a solo reading! If he could bore us to hysteria in fifteen minutes, imagine what he could do to us in sixty! The truth is, for all our trigger-happy anarchy, we were a pretty malleable and insouciant bunch and amenable to just about anything that looked like it had the possibility of being even marginally entertaining.

So Jackson came back the next week and gave his solo reading. This time there were five or six interminable poems, one as pointlessly random as the next. When someone walked in in the middle of one of his pieces, letting a cold blast of winter into the coffee house, Jackson said "Please shut the door," but in so much the same voice and without missing a beat that it was a moment or two before it dawned on me, on any of us, that the phrase wasn't in the poem—or rather hadn't been in the poem—until he'd uttered it. The perimeters of the poem had simply shifted to include that chance remark. A Mac Low poem, it suddenly became clear, wasn't a closed system. The process and content were interconnected in some mysterious and intriguing way. A Mac Low poem was, in fact, something entirely different from the sort of thing I was used to.

It knocked me over. I'd never heard anything like it. In one fell swoop, Jackson Mac Low had laid waste several centuries of prohibitions and had shifted the boundaries of poetry for me—and no doubt for many others. It was a wonderful reading, boring as hell and utterly exhilarating. Immediately, everyone took to writing Jackson Mac Low poems: aelotropic concoctions based on chance operations. We wrote dictionary poems, poems based on intricate mathematical systems and formulas. We cut in phrases from the Kabala, the Mahabharata, the Sunday comics, the Congressional Record. It was all grist for the mill. We'd choose fourteen words at random from the OED, count the number of letters, and if there were 63, let's say, we'd simply turn to page 63 of *The Secret of the Golden Flower,* copy down the first seven words in the first 37 lines and use six of those words in one line, three in the next, and so on. The whole business was great fun. I don't imagine it generated much in the way of immortal poetry but it had the virtue of being a cut, slash, and burn operation on the sequential and conventionally rational—an incendiary device to stick under the language so we could watch it explode—words and phrases flying like shrapnel all the hell over the place. Now that the sonnet and villanelle were safely buried in university lit departments, this new pipe-bomb formalism was just what we needed to take up the slack. Mac Low—a student, friend, and disciple of John Cage—was liberating us as radically as Ginsberg had with *Howl* and Burroughs had with his cut-up concoctions in *The Naked Lunch.*

A few months later Mickey closed the *Tenth Street* and opened *Le Deux Megots.* It was four times the size and the place caught on almost at once—the loyal following from the old *Tenth Street* being joined by scores of new poets and poetry groupies. The weekly open readings became a New York literary institution. On the evenings of those open readings there'd be a formidable mob haunting the place. They'd be outside lounging around on parked cars, smoking and bullshitting, making dope deals and pickups: an assortment of hustlers, hoodlums, deadbeats, artists, students, bongo players, hipsters, and out-and-out sociopaths—the greasy, zit-ridden habitués of late-night donut shops and 24-hour cafeterias. A fair proportion of the *demimonde* young women could be relied upon to show up in black leather, one taut face paler than the next. There were cadaverous poets of both sexes and several in between. The one thing they all had in common was a secret back-pocket manuscript or tattered spring binder filled with language. Notebooks full of rage, alienation, and despair: They were waiting their turn, sprawled against parked cars biding their time before the open reading began: lumpen-nihilists working themselves up for their five-minute rant against cosmological betrayal and the tumescent vagina of beatitude's marmoreal lips.

Donald Allen's provocatively anti-mainstream anthology *The New American Poetry* had not been published yet—as I remember—but the careful craftsmen and new traditionalists were on showcase in that little Hall-Pack-Simpson anthology, *The New Poets of England and America.* Those post-Auden poets, albeit bone-dry and middle class to a fault, were an impressive lot. Lowell in Boston, Larkin in England, and several dozen others were writing in a mid-twentieth century idiom that was elegant, ironic, passionate, formal, and beautifully wrought. One evening, sipping my hot chocolate, I overheard Bob Kelly lecturing some of his coterie on the unpleasantness of that anthology. He was predictably disdainful. He intimated there wasn't a poem in the whole collection that was worth reading. All that rear-guard formalism, those deadly iambs! There was truth, of course, in what he was saying. Still and all, there were real beauties in that book that weren't so easy to dismiss. Poems that anyone could see were splendid pieces of work. I'd been carrying my copy around for the past couple of months, poring over it with the most intense interest.

I pulled my well-thumbed copy out of my satchel, opened it to Snodgrass's "April Inventory," walked over to Kelly's table and said "Here, read this!" A somewhat impulsive gesture considering that I hardly knew the fellow. In fact I regretted it the moment I'd done it. Kelly examined the poem silently. You could see by the tilt of his eyebrow that he wasn't pleased. I might just as well have stuck a piece of chewed bubblegum into his hand. When he was done he handed the piece of dead gum back to me without a word—Imperially—and returned to his cruller. Kelly was a formidable presence, and not simply because of his astonishing girth. Already teaching at Bard, he had taken on the manner of a literary savant, a kind of poor man's Edmund Wilson—though he probably imagined it was Pound whose mantle he had inherited. Kelly was co-editing *Trobar* with Jerry Rothenberg, who was an utterly unpretentious and likeable fellow, and writing hermetic little "deep-image" couplets, poems of an admirably polished surface and the post-modern predilection for impenetrability. Anyone who doesn't think there are armed camps in American poetry doesn't know what the fuck he's talking about.

The General's Son: Journey of an Israeli in Palestine, A Memoir by Miko Peled

The author of this engaging and important memoir is a sixth-degree black belt who runs a thriving karate school in Coronado. He is also the son of one of Israel's most notable generals and political dissidents, Matti Peled, a war hero who shocked Israel several decades ago by becoming a vocal peace advocate and a professor of Arabic literature at Tel Aviv University.

The author's mother seems to have been no less a remarkable figure: In 1948, after several hundred thousand Palestinian civilians had been forced to flee, never to be permitted to return, she refused to follow the example of her compatriots and expropriate the abandoned home of a dispossessed family. She is quoted many years later as explaining: "That I should take the home of a family that may be living in a refugee camp? The home of another mother. . . . I refused. . . . And to see the Israelis driving away with loot, beautiful rugs and furniture, I was ashamed for them. I don't know how they could do it."

Even as a young man, the author, a proud Israeli patriot, encounters a number of disquieting realities. Shortly after he is drafted in 1980, the members of his elite commando unit are instructed by their commanding officer to walk up and down the streets of Ramallah in the West Bank and "if anyone so much as looked at us, we were to... 'break every bone in their body.'" At another point, the author recalls an Israeli naval commando casually describing how his unit would torture and drown Gaza fishermen "to teach the Arabs who was boss."

But the author's real journey of awakening comes after his beloved 13-year-old niece, Smadar, is killed by a suicide bomber on a Tel Aviv street. Smadar's father, Miko's brother-in law, begins devoting himself to the Bereaved Families Forum, an organization of Jewish and Palestinian parents who have lost children to the conflict, while Nurit, Smadar's mother and Miko's sister, begins speaking and writing about the need to stop the bloodbath—for which work, in 2001, she was awarded the Sacharov Prize for Freedom of Thought from the European Parliament.

Not long after Smadar's tragic death, Miko, who had already moved with his wife Gila to the United States, finds himself at a Jewish-Palestinian dialogue group in San Diego, and among Palestinians for the first time in his life. There, to his astonishment, he finds Jewish and Palestinian-Americans laughing together and treating each other as friends and equals. From the Palestinians in the group, he tells us, "I heard stories of displacement and ruthlessness I had never imagined possible."

Traveling between Israel and the United States, the author continues to learn unpleasant truths, and, by reading Israeli historians such as Ilan Pappé and Avi Schlaim, he begins to understand that the exculpatory explanations for the Palestinian mass exodus of 1948 are largely a collection of myths.

Miko and his Palestinian-American friend Nader Elbanna, a fellow Rotarian—a man who had grown up in a refugee camp in Jordan after his family had been forced to flee their home in the 1948 expulsion—begin giving talks to Rotary Clubs about the Israeli conflict and Palestinian dispossession. Eventually, the two men raise enough money to buy a thousand wheelchairs, half of which they earmark for needy Israelis and the other half for needy Palestinians. By this point, the reader is not entirely surprised to learn that Israel resists permitting those 500 wheelchairs to reach a Palestinian hospital. After finally managing to deliver them, the two friends arrive at a checkpoint, where Miko is harassed and threatened with arrest and finally experiences for himself, "the humiliation thousands of Palestinians have to go through every day."

Given the accumulation of such experiences, it should not be surprising that the author, a member of one of Israel's most notable families, arrives at the conviction that genuine democracy for both Israelis and Palestinians is the only real solution to the conflict, and that Palestinians and Jews must "live in one state where we are completely equal in every way."

For anyone wishing to understand the complex dynamics of one of the world's most consequential and tragic conflicts, Miko Peled's courageous, revelatory, and compassionate memoir, *The General's Son*, is likely to become required reading.

Radicals, Rabbis and Peacemakers: Conversations with Jewish Critics of Israel, edited by Seth Farber

In the Jewish-American community one can exhibit complete indifference to Jewish culture and be an outspoken atheist and yet remain a perfectly acceptable member of the tribe. On the other hand, any Jew who openly disapproves of the State of Israel is at risk of being branded a traitor, a dupe of the ubiquitous anti-Semitic enemy, and a self-loathing Jew. Most of the writers and activists represented in Seth Farber's *Radicals, Rabbis and Peacemakers* are unapologetic anti-Zionists, and thus "traitors" in precisely that most honorable sense.

Farber's book, lively and provocative, reflects not only the author's commitment to social justice, but [also], according to a brief biographical note, "his faith in prophetic Judaism as a medium of spiritual/social transformation." So these conversations serve a dual purpose: on the one hand they explore the Palestinian/Israeli struggle from a progressive Jewish point of view and, on the other, they engage the question of contemporary Judaism itself, a post-Holocaust faith that has largely replaced the love of Yahweh with the worship of Israel.

Noam Chomsky, in his conversation with the author, asserts that the very concept of a state that is not the state of its citizens but of the Jewish people is an illegitimate principle upon which to have founded the nation of Israel. He clarifies his advocacy of the two-state solution by explaining that he conceives such a political configuration to be no more than a stepping stone toward a binational state, but just how the creation of a tiny Palestinian state can lead to Israel and Palestine becoming a single binational nation Chomsky does not make clear, and it is not impossible that his current position reflects his own ambivalence about that issue. He also hedges his bet on the right of return: the Palestinians must not be forced to give up that right, he declares, "but the expectation that it will be implemented is completely unrealistic. And to advocate that is just to cause pain and disaster to the refugees." Although this is a common enough position among progressive Zionists, it is much the sort of logic Alice encountered after tumbling down the rabbit hole. In similar fashion, Chomsky admits that the Jews had no more right to establish a state on land that was not theirs than did the American colonists, but then dismisses this most sticky and fundamental of issues with the casual comment that he doesn't "see a lot of point in these discussions."

Joel Kovel, author and former psychoanalyst, is less equivocal: "Zionism is a horrible mistake." Israel is illegitimate in much the way Apartheid South Africa was illegitimate. Because of its privileging of one racial group above others, it is not capable of "joining the community of nation states that are grounded in universal human rights." Nor does Kovel have a particularly high opinion of ancient Judaism, observing that despite the "transcendent ethical potential" of its beliefs, ancient Judaism had "not just a sense of superiority but a rejection of everybody else."

Adam Shapiro, one of the founders of the International Solidarity Movement, who became momentarily newsworthy in the United States when his parents were threatened by outraged Brooklyn Zionists, observes that "any anti-Semitism that you find in Muslim countries today is the direct result of the policies of Israel vis-à-vis Palestinians." When Farber suggests how ironic it is that the Jews turned into oppressors, Shapiro replies that he does not find it at all surprising. "Over and over and over in human history those who have been oppressed have turned into the oppressors." And when Farber suggests that something in Jewish ethical tradition might have kept them moral for all those centuries, Shapiro reminds him that those supposed Jewish values are nowhere in evidence in those colorful biblical stories in which various peoples are exterminated by the pious Hebrews under God's mandate.

Phyllis Bennis, author of *Calling the Shots: How Washington Dominates Today's UN*, reminds us of something that is rarely acknowledged: even if the three-quarters of a million Palestinians had fled in 1948 at the bequest of the Arab invaders, as the Israeli version of history had for so long insisted, "those refugees still would have the right to go home.

It doesn't matter the reason they fled. Their right to return is not conditional on having fled for the right reason." Bennis also makes the important point that the U.S. Mobilization for Peace and Justice, by making opposition to U.S. support for Israeli occupation a central component at its mass anti-war demonstrations, has helped break through the solid wall of U.S. support for Israeli aggression.

Another conversation is with Steve Quester, an activist with the New York organization Jews Against the Occupation who remarks, in a fascinating aside, that being queer allowed him to figure out that everything he'd been taught about Israel was a lie: "Whereas for straight Jews who've never gone through this process of realizing that they've been systematically lied to by all aspects of the society, it's much harder for them to let go of all the lies they've been taught about Israel."

Another conversation is with Ora Wise, the passionately outspoken daughter of a "very Zionist" Conservative rabbi, a young woman who worked with Rabbis for Human Rights in the West Bank and was a founding member of the Ohio State Committee for Justice in Palestine. Dealing head on with the criticism that the Palestinians should organize non-violent resistance, she reminds us that terrorist attacks are "the product of a brutal, vicious, controlling, oppressive military occupation that is destroying the lives of millions of Palestinians and is deliberately destroying Palestinians' ability to organize in non-violent ways. . . ."

The conversation with Norman Finkelstein, perhaps, by now, the most famous Jewish-American critic of Zionist machinations, is peppered with statements by various eyewitnesses to Israeli crimes and with chilling remarks by such luminaries as Moshe Dayan and David Ben-Gurion and is followed by a brief essay by Finkelstein on Israel and Zionism. Finkelstein's discussion of Israeli "race-nationalism" in particular, and Zionist ideology in general, is sharply focused and forceful, in that incendiary, take-no-prisoners polemic style that makes his own books such a sizzling read. When Farber quotes to Finkelstein a remark by the Jewish theologian Marc Ellis, to the effect that those

Jews struggling for Palestinian rights "may ultimately decide the future of the covenant. . . and the Jewish people," Finkelstein dismisses the notion saying "I have no interest in covenants. I don't know who the Jewish people are. These are all metaphysical, extraneous terms for me."

But they are not extraneous for Farber. Rather, for him, they are absolutely central. To focus on such questions, Farber has chosen to include conversations with Norton Mezvinsky, an advocate of the Universalist humanism promoted by early Reform Judaism, and with two orthodox Jewish thinkers: Daniel Boyarin and Rabbi David Weiss, both of whom are anti-Zionists.

Mezvinsky, who was singled out by Daniel Pipes' Campus Watch for "spewing anti-Semitic calumnies," is another who believes that Zionism is inherently a racist ideology. On the matter of the two-state solution, he argues that what the Israeli leadership has always meant by a Palestinian state is a small "autonomous region" without any real sovereignty. Considering that 40% of the water for all Israel comes from aquifers the Israelis have built in the West Bank, it is hardly likely, he argues, that they will return the West Bank to the Palestinians. If neither a single state nor two genuine states is currently realistic, why not opt, Mezvinsky suggests, for the better, more democratic and just approach—a binational state.

The two orthodox Jews have a difficult time squaring their hatred of Israel's military aggression with their biblical literalism. Though Daniel Boyarin believes that Zionism is "out-and-out heresy," he is clearly uncomfortable when Farber reminds him of Yahweh's commands that the Israelites commit genocide against various peoples. He insists that such questions are simply "not relevant anymore," though clearly, if one is a literalist, they are indeed relevant. When Farber poses the same sort of question to David Weiss, a rabbi of the Neturie Karta community, the rabbi can only fumble helplessly in response:

But it's not my issue to try to answer for G-d why he would want such a thing which is in the bible which is accepted. I could look and try to find, according to the Kabbalah, reasons, you know. . . that's secret as far as, you know, there's a deeper meaning for everything. . .

For Weiss, the reestablishment of Jewish legitimacy over the holy land is a perfectly legitimate goal—so long as it occurs after the return of the Messiah.

If Farber's least favorite Jewish progressive is Rabbi Michael Lerner, who has famously argued that Jews had the right to steal the Palestinian homeland as an act of "affirmative action," the figure whose position the author most fully seems to respect is the theologian and philosopher Marc Ellis, who apparently refused or was unable to participate in this project. Farber has included a brief essay by Ellis and has made that author the subject of both his introductory and concluding essays. Like Mezvinsky, Ellis advocates a Jewish theology of liberation based on the tradition of the later prophets and is opposed to "Constantinian Judaism," the notion that the secular power of a national state is the true fulfillment of the Jewish covenant. His is another variation of Reform Judaism's early but long abandoned commitment to universal brotherhood.

It would have been useful for Common Courage Press to have hired a decent copyeditor to correct the shocking number of distracting typos and help the author organize the material a bit more gracefully. The conversations seem to have been transcribed to the page unedited, interviewer and interviewee constantly—and at times disconcertingly—interrupting one other. A good editing of the individual conversations would have helped. Those caveats aside, for anyone seriously interested in the question of Zionism, Israeli colonialism, and the Palestinian struggle, *Radicals, Rabbis and Peacemakers* will be a provocative and absorbing read. The complexity and richness of the discussions are not the least of the book's virtues. And for those struggling with the issue of how believing Jews can frame their faith and confront the disconcerting issues of Israeli aggression and Zionist supremacism, it will prove doubly provocative and doubly a pleasure.

[From "The First Noble Truth"]

They loved Siddhartha. No surprises there! But when I pick up
the chalk & scratch on the board *DUKKA: The First*
Noble Truth: Suffering permeates life, no one looks pleased. . .

—from the title poem in Kowit's book by the same name

Poetic & Political Potpourri

Checkers   Mary Reed

Terry Hertzler

The Chiron Interview
(Summer 2004)

Steve Kowit was born and raised in Brooklyn, New York, and has lived on the West Coast for the past 27 years or so. He came of age during the Lower East Side coffee-house poetry-reading scene of the early 1960s, moved to Haight-Ashbury and lived there until the Vietnam War heated up, and then fled with his wife to Mexico and parts south. He's editor and publisher of *The Maverick Poets*, author of *In the Palm of Your Hand: The Poet's Portable Workshop,* and a handful of collections of poetry, most recently *The Dumbbell Nebula*. He is recipient of an NEA fellowship and a Pushcart Prize, as well as other awards. An incorrigible loudmouth and political activist, he founded the first animal-rights organization in San Diego in the '80s, and last year wrote the introduction for *We the Creatures*, an anthology of contemporary animal-rights poetry. His essay on the Xhosa mass suicide in the mid-19th century as a model of collective self-deception, will be published in *Skeptic Magazine*. He's taught on the West Coast for the past two decades and lives with his beloved wife Mary, and several dogs and cats, in the back-country hills of San Diego County near the Mexican border. He was interviewed by Terry Hertzler, Vietnam combat veteran, fellow San Diego poet, publisher of Caernarvon Press, and an old friend.

TERRY HERTZLER: You seem to enjoy teaching and are clearly much sought after, your serious students coming back again and again. Your classes are always fun and lively. What is your approach to teaching?

STEVE KOWIT: Yeah, teaching poetry is fun because I'm constantly using models of poems I love and I tend to draw fine students—people whom I have lots of respect for. Many are old friends since people tend to take the class several times. There are people who've been studying with me, off and on, for twenty years. When I'm most awake, I know that I really don't know more than my students about the world, that I haven't any right to pretend to be superior. They're my equals and many students sitting in any classroom are brighter than I am and know a great deal more than I do about all sorts of things. I want the environment to be friendly and fun, and I don't want to play the role of the expert or the teacher. I learned some basic things about teaching from the Church of Scientology, things about communication and listening well and acknowledging the communication coming from the person with whom you're speaking. I studied Scientology for about three years. Intensively. It was my life for those three years. I have very mixed feelings about much of it. It is not a trustworthy practice; it's coercive and rather stupidly self-righteous. Hubbard was more than a bit of an ass, and I wouldn't recommend it—but some of the data is wonderful.

Over all, I think it's important to love your students, to feel great warmth and affection and friendship for them—I think it's clear to my students that I respect them as equals and peers, that I love poetry, that I love craft, that I love a phrase or a word that says what needs to be said with precision, that almost audible click that Yeats talks about—and that I'm delighted to be with them, sharing what little I know. And I make sure they understand that I'm often wrong-headed and they shouldn't believe everything I say—that there are no rules, only cases. That anyone can write a marvelous poem out of any aesthetic theory. That there's simply no one right way to do it. I remind them that I am often teaching out of my own prejudices. When my class is working, everyone is laughing and having a good time and feels that this is just where they want to be. I try to do that same thing in my teaching manual *In the Palm of Your Hand: The Poet's Portable Workshop*. What I think I convey, at least when I'm on, is that the whole thing is gloriously good fun, that it's nothing but a delectable game, and yet that writing is also, at the same time, a high spiritual exercise. Ultimately, after questions of skill and verbal deftness have been considered, it's the depth of the spirit, the level of moral and psychological trustworthiness that writers need. It's the depth from which the emotions and perceptions spring that counts. Whitman once observed to Horace Traubel that if a writer doesn't like women or feels he has a right to be waited upon, or has some other meanness or character flaw, it will show up in his poetry. Yes! How deep is the life from which the work springs? That's the final question.

You know, there are people who naively imagine that you can get rid of ego in poetry by dropping the use of the word "I"—that the word "I" presents a problem in contemporary poetry—that confessional or personal poetry is somehow limited because of that "I." Seems ridiculous. Acknowledging the "I" and using it strategically to say what you want to say has nothing to do with the problem of ego, has nothing whatsoever to do with the problem of the small, self-aggrandizing self as it gets in the way of the poem and makes it smaller, narrower, less generous than it ought to have been. Of course, that means I'm interested in what a poem is saying, not just how it's said. A decidedly anti-modernist altitude. If it marks me as hopelessly out of sync with the times, that's fine with me, too.

TH: I know that you've been influenced by a number of spiritual teachers, people such as L. Ron Hubbard, whom you just mentioned, as well as Werner Erhard, Bhagwan Shree Rajneesh, and George Gurdjieff, each of whom seems to have had rather questionable aspects to their character. Do those experiences have anything to do with your sense of yourself as a skeptic, a person who—however much you are interested in spiritual issues and meditative paths—is no longer easily captivated by spiritual systems and metaphysical beliefs? I'm thinking, too, of your manuscript concerning collective self-deception. What part does all that play in your poetry?

SK: Yes, I suppose it does. I spent six years working on that book about self-deception, a book that might never, at least in its entirety, be published. But I learned a great deal. It crystallized certain feelings I had about the central flaw in the human mind—and why we're such a fucked-up species. People love to believe! Believe anything! My childhood was in part shaped by the Nuremberg War Crimes trials and the revelations of the Holocaust, those eugenics beliefs that various races were congenitally evil or greedy or murderous or untrustworthy.

FDR believed the Japanese were sneaky by nature—exactly the same belief that the German "scientists" had about Jews and Gypsies.

When I was in the 7th grade, way back in the Joe MaCarthy '50s, I refused to pledge my allegiance to the American flag. And around that same time I was shocked to find out that the new "beloved" state of Israel (I come from a big Jewish family) was a state in which Jews had more rights than other people, and I sensed, though I was still a naive kid, that something didn't smell right about that. I mean if Hitler's Aryan State was a murderous idea, why was the idea of a Jewish state going to be any better? And, as it turned out, my instincts were right. For more than half a century the U.S. press and government have instructed the populace to believe that the European Jews who stole the Palestinian homeland have a perfect right to what is now called Israel, and that the millions of Palestinians who have been expelled from their homes don't exist or are subhuman terrorists.

A decade later, in my twenties, I refused to fight in Vietnam. I was in the reserves because the Coney Island Draft Board had refused to allow me to become a conscientious objector, and when I moved to San Francisco in '67 I sent the Army a letter of resignation telling them I'd never put that uniform on again. The Vietnam War taught me about the horrors of American self-righteousness—and how all the stuff I'd learned about the American love of democracy around the world was nothing but convenient mythology fed to a citizenry willing to believe what they were told—over and over and over. Chomsky says, "It is easy to come to believe what we find convenient to believe." Amen.

I was wonderfully and woefully disillusioned on several occasions in my spiritual search, and those experiences also helped shape me. As I've already suggested, Hubbard and Scientology were not, in the long run, trustworthy, although I learned a tremendous amount from that practice and am very grateful to the Church of Scientology for that. I was in the Gurdjieff Work for a few years, but Gurdjieff himself was clearly an aberrant fellow with a puffed-up sense of himself and a lot of his speculative metaphysical stuff seems to me to be laughable nonsense. Nonetheless, I learned a great deal from the Gurdjieff Work, too, and still feel attached to it, and still use the central fourth-way meditation of trying throughout the day to wake up. Ouspensky's *The Fourth Way* was a real guide for me as far back as my late teens, long before I entered the Gurdjieff Work.

Werner Erhard's EST training became enormously useful in my life. I learned a great deal from it, too, and, as I did in Scientology, had some important opening experiences there. Transformative experiences. Whether Werner fondled his daughters one night in a hotel I can't say. On the other hand, some of the EST philosophy was pernicious bullshit. The notion that we're totally responsible for everything that happens to us. No. Not at all. Gurdjieff was much more correct on that one. He said we lived under the "Law of Accident" and that, in fact, we controlled a great deal less of our decisions and choices and behavior than we imagined. Erhart—who had been a Scientologist for many years—would have us believe that cancer patients somehow induce their own cancer. They have to take responsibility for their cancer. That's just low-level, new-age mystical malarkey.

I practiced Zen rigorously for several years after I left the Gurdjieff Work. But, as it turns out, my Zen teacher, Maezumi Roshi, a fine, lovely man, was an alcoholic who had an eye for 13-year-old girls. His senior students finally got him into an alcohol treatment program in San Diego and the teenybopper sex—Jesus, you can go to prison for a long time for that sort of stuff—was hushed up. I think all that pretty much ended my Zen practice. My other wonderful Zen teacher, Thich Thien-An, a marvelous, gentle man, had died in his fifties of a brain tumor a few years before, and in those last months it seemed to me that he was clearly distracted, scared, upset—just like anyone would be in that situation. So it seemed clear that spiritual practice didn't entirely stave off the suffering, the horrible tragedy, or even the fear of death. But Zen practice, a rigorous daily sitting practice, changed my life. It was wonderful. I don't recommend half-lotus: it's bad for the back and awful for the knees. But a daily dose of zazen—shutting up the mind—was wonderful therapy. Perhaps the most transformative experience came as a result of the EST Training. There was a wonderful process late in the training when I was forced to confront eating animals, and what we do to animals every day in order to satisfy our palates, the inexpressible misery that innocent animals suffer, in slaughterhouses and medical laboratories, the vast, unspeakable horrors that we all silently assent to so that we can have our rib roasts and veal cutlets. That was a great shock to my system.

At the time I was working on the opening Koan, Joshu's Mu, "Do dogs have Buddha Nature?" Oddly, I don't remember who gave me that Koan. Not Maezumi because he was a Soto Zen teacher. It must have been some Renzai teacher I sat with at one time—I don't recall. But the practice was powerful—though maybe not in the way intended. What came home to me every day was the casual cruelty of human beings. How could we be in such profound denial? That's the central issue I guess. Out of that grief and horror I started an Animal Rights organization here in San Diego. That murderous nature, without the slightest guilt, is central to who we are as a species. Even given the vast amount of torture and killing for fun in which U.S. troops indulged in Vietnam, the massive bombing of that country, the bombing of the civilian cities of Hiroshima and Nagasaki, our daily war crimes in Iraq, our continual invasion and occupation of other countries, our continual support for right-wing dictatorships and disdain for democratic movements around the world, our very recent overthrow of the Aristide democracy in Haiti—most Americans still imagine their country to be righteous and peace-loving. It's almost beyond belief, the degree to which people can deceive themselves.

People believe what they want to, evidence or no evidence. Our beloved holy books are blatantly malignant. Yahweh was, generally speaking, a sociopathic deity infatuated with genocide, a partisan of slavery and rape, and his Israelite people were the cruelest, most savage—and sanctimonious—of barbarians. A supremacist, slave-owning, warlike people, intent on stealing the Middle East from its inhabitants. What they bequeathed to Christianity was that sanctimonious, supremacist philosophy. And the Christian Scriptures, ironically, turned the tables and became little more than an anti-Jewish polemic—Jesus curses the Jews as children of the Devil, and the authors of the Gospels have the Jews call down a curse upon their own heads. I don't know if Mel Gibson is, like his father, an anti-Semite, but the crucifixion as represented in the Gospels is largely an anti-Jewish polemic. Those Christian scriptures lead from St. John Chrysostom and Augustine's anti-Jewish rants directly to the pogroms of the Middle Ages, the expulsion of the Jews from various countries, and, finally, to the smokestacks of Auschwitz.

Then, too, there are other monstrously destructive elements in Christianity. Jesus says what any spoiled, narcissistic adolescent would say: "If you don't agree with me, you will go to hell and suffer eternal torment!" Threatening eternal suffering to those who don't agree with you is the single most sadistic philosophy you will find in any religion. If people don't like what Jesus suffers on the cross in Gibson's film, imagine what an unbeliever suffers throughout eternity in the Christian hell. This is the god of love? And those two vicious texts are the sacred books of the West! They're Hitlerian! Both of those malignant books should be discarded, abandoned, forgotten. . . .

You know, Terry, I've always had the feeling that monotheism is far more dangerous than polytheism because it says, "There is but one God—and we've got him!" Well, I won't go on. In the end, my sense— my very deep sense—is that we are not who we think we are—the tribal nature of *Homo satanicus* is murderous. Social animals are the only ones who are capable of warfare and we are, of course, far and away the species with the greatest degree of inter-tribal cooperation. That means the species that is apt to be most warlike. E. O. Wilson says there are ant species that are even more warlike than man, but I have a hard time believing it. Our religions are self-aggrandizing, small-minded reflections of our pitiable congenital meanness and inherent thirst for blood. Somewhere, Simone Weil says she never met a soldier who didn't relish killing. Man's impulse for murdering the "other" is an absolutely central part of his nature. It has nothing to do with economic oppression or capitalism. The role of all this in my poetry? I think in the past few years it's shown up more and more—I write a lot of political poetry these days—though my interest earlier in the silliness of the human ego—a theme that enters into a good deal of my poetry—is suggestive, perhaps, of that direction.

TH: You are clearly interested in what a poem is saying, not just how it says it. Some poets and poetry workshop teachers would claim that poetry is subjective and intuitive, and different readers will take entirely different meanings from the same poem—that a poem might be complex, nonlinear, multilayered, and difficult, or that an author may not always know what a poem might mean to others—that the meaning a person gets from a poem might even be something of a revelation to the author, that how a poem says what it says, no matter how complex or ambiguous or indeterminate the poem is, is what counts. How do you respond to that?

SK: Much of that is an excuse for the great self-indulgence of the reigning aesthetic, the idea of the surreal or deep image, the "intuitive, just-let-it-happen, trust yourself completely" sort of poem that wells up, putatively, from so deep a place in the psyche that even the poet doesn't know what he's saying. Well, maybe at times that does happen and produces a successful poem. Far more often the poet loses control of his material and his end product comes to nothing but a huge yawn from the hapless reader. The problem is that the image and narrative are too shallow rather than too deep. There's that wonderfully amusing Billy Collins poem about students wanting to tie a poem to a chair and beat a confession out of it. But in fact, Billy Collins, a superb poet, is almost always deliciously clear to a decent reader. His poems don't need to be tied to a chair and beaten into a confession. Lots of poems that can mean all sorts of things really don't mean much of anything. I think, overall, that complex, difficult, multi-layered, nonlinear poetry is a long series of failed experiments.

The question of a poet's intentions came up in my creative writing class a while ago, a couple of students suggesting how hard it is to separate what they'd intended to say from what the reader gets, because the communication is already fleshed out in the writer's head. So they had the illusion that they had managed to transfer that information to the page. When they laughed about that insight, a number of their classmates were nodding affirmatively. They'd had the same experience: their poems hadn't conveyed what they'd thought they had.

It seems to me absolutely essential to let the writers in workshops know how much of their intention in a piece under discussion was realized. What's the good of having marvelous verbal, musical, and imaginative skills if you can't say what you had wished to—or are deluded into imagining you've said something clearly when you've left everyone in soporific confusion? Often a poet thinks he's written a poem about, say, his grandmother and the horrors of war, and eight workshop participants will swear that the poem is about cloud formations, six are certain it's about the Virgin of Guadalupe, and the rest suspect it's a paean to chopped liver. I would guess that you can go to the authors of more than half of the thoroughly incoherent poems published in any collection of literary journals and learn that those writers have no doubt whatsoever that their poems are perfectly intelligible—if only the reader had been more alert, knew a little more about reading serious poetry! Blaming the reader is commonplace among contemporary poets, especially poets of the incoherent persuasion.

TH: Speaking of Billy Collins, why do you think there was so much controversy when he was named Poet Laureate of the United States a few years back?

SK: Collins is a wonderful and wonderfully popular poet. He's one of the few who's read by lots of people who aren't so-called "serious students of poetry." His books actually sell. He's completely intelligible and therefore is far outside the mainstream aesthetic which cherishes poems no one can understand, and which the critics and professors can have a field day "explicating." So Collins, who can be understood by any decent reader—and understood on a first reading, and whose work is amusing and entertaining and fun—is much resented. He's a threat! Sharon Olds was resented for the same reason when she was a rising star. People read her who didn't major in literary theory! I've actually read poet critics saying explicitly that poems that can be understood on a first reading are not worth reading! My god, no wonder no one reads the stuff!

As far as I'm concerned, poetry has to be as readable, as pleasurable, as delightful, and as accessible as any other kind of literature—as a good short story or vignette or essay or memoir: Dylan Thomas's "Do Not Go Gentle" might have a few knotty lines, but it is basically perfectly intelligible. Elizabeth Bishop's "One Art" is perfectly intelligible. Larkin's "Aubade" and "Church Going" are perfectly intelligible. The early, pre-*Patterson* Williams is often wonderfully intelligible. Marvelous poetry! So I'm not advocating some sort of simple-minded poetic. Ron Koertge and Billy Collins are as sophisticated as any writers around. Dorianne Laux and Kim Addonizio, two marvelous contemporaries who are among the very best and most exciting, are "complex" poets, but poets who always make sure they're intelligible. Mary Oliver, that marvelous poet who comes as close to an enlightened vision as any American of our period, is thoroughly intelligible. Poems that aren't intelligible seem to me to be flawed in an essential way. They are unlikely to do what literature has to do to be ultimately successful. Hart Crane notwithstanding, the defining characteristic of language, after all, is communicability. By rights, many of the so-called Language Poets should be called Anti-Language Poets. So too the more "difficult" of the academics.

But that doesn't mean intelligibility is the only criterion of effective poetry. It's usually a necessary condition but never a sufficient one. There are journals chock full of intelligible poems that are boring, unambitious, self-aggrandizing, poorly crafted, musically inept, and uninteresting. The Bukowski school produced untold numbers of would-be Buks and untold numbers of mediocre poems. Most of them about pussy and beer. Adolescent machismo poems. Indeed, Bukowski himself rarely brought off—to my taste—a splendidly memorable poem. He was a terrific talent and in one sense very therapeutic because he insisted on writing intelligibly. He had a fine ear for the American idiom and was a consistently engaging storyteller. I don't at all mean to demean or dismiss him. In one sense, out of his work, came one branch of the exciting poetry being produced today. He and Ed

Field and poets like Ron Koertge helped change the poetic landscape, showed others how to write a kind of poetry that was nothing like the high modernist stuff that was coming out of the Wallace Stevens New Critical sensibility that dominated American poetry for so long. Of course, early Williams was terrific in that same sense: he was writing perfectly understandable and marvelously constructed poems in the ordinary language. Poems in which every syllable was just right!

And that's not to mention Ray Carver, a superb model. When he was at his best he was writing poetry of the highest order. And then there's Jeffers, a towering figure, too serious to "play" with language. Jeffers represented poetry at its most classical, most serious, most lyrically austere. I love—isn't it obvious—poets who speak a human language, who have no truck with fashion, who want to speak their piece. Carver said "No tricks" and that's what he meant: no rhetorical cutenesses, no moves that are merely clever. A poet doesn't wish to be admired, Cocteau said, but believed.

Back to teaching, just let me say that it's very therapeutic for a workshop participant to know whether an audience of attentive readers gets what she's saying. This has nothing whatsoever to do with the issues of intentional ambiguity and thematic complexity, or the fact that images and scenes can resonate widely and encompass a wide spectrum of implications. If a poem can mean anything the reader wants it to mean, then it doesn't mean much of anything. Those workshop participants who are high modernists and postmodernists and don't want to say anything intelligible in their poems, who don't want their poems to contain anything so vulgar as a "meaning," can take heart from such workshop sessions in the realization that their offering remained impenetrably opaque and successfully glazed the eyes of just about everyone who'd managed to remain awake—exactly as they'd intended!

TH: What do you think of the popularity of "spoken word" poetry and "slam" poetry—the idea of poetry as competition?

SK: Interesting phenomena. Those venues are where the non-white, non-middle class, non-academic poets hang out. It's a different sound: part street, part rap and hip-hop, all of it feisty and sassy. Maybe too much attitude and too little hard rewriting. But that's where you hear most of the real political poetry nowadays. Rarely in the pages of the mainstream lit journals or at university poetry readings or in the usual anthologies. The spoken-word venues are where the black and Puerto Rican and Hispanic poets of social consciousness are presenting their work. I grew up with the Lower East Side poetry scene in New York and those endless open readings had much the same feel as the spoken-word stuff that is being performed today in cities all over the country to rather surprisingly large and enthusiastic live audiences. Lots of excitement. Always a kind of party at those places. The bohemian equivalent of the pick-up bar: lots of good-looking young poets on the make. Of course, it's still largely an audience of fellow poets. I've only been to one slam, in Phoenix I think it was, and it turned out to be a lot of fun and done very well, done sensitively so that no one got hurt. Of course, much of the work isn't brilliant, and some of it is laughably dreadful and unskilled, but then neither is most of the work coming out of the mainstream particularly luminous or masterful. These scenes have, at least, a raw energy that hasn't been polished out of existence. My only complaint is that those open readings are endless, often go on for hours, and there's just so much one can take. But there are fine talents there, too. People like Quincy Troupe. I heard Manny Ortiz read his wonderful long political poem "A Moment of Silence" before about 150 people in Claire de Lune, a well-known poetry coffee-house in San Diego last year. Many of the participants are young and learning their craft. Some will become marvelous poets. Wonderful! More power to that scene!

TH: You mentioned that much of your current writing addresses politics in one way or another. There was a slogan in the 1960s: "Everything Is Political." Do you believe that is true, and if so, how do you think that affects (or should affect) poetry today?

SK: I think it was something that poets said who were embarrassed to be writing poems that were not at all political. An easy way to get themselves off the hook. In the past three years we have bombed Afghanistan, killed thousands of innocent people, crippled and wounded tens of thousands, and replaced the Taliban with the despised Northern Alliance. We invaded Iraq, have already killed tens of thousands of innocent people there, put tens of thousands in prison, and pretty much destroyed their society—this after 10 years of illegal bombing—mostly by a Democratic Party administration—bombing that took the lives of well over a million civilians mostly by destroying their water purification facilities. We just invaded Haiti a couple of weeks ago in order to throw out the first democratically elected president of that country—a man who refused to play ball with the U.S. heavy-money agenda. So that we can again control Haiti for the sake of U.S. corporate interests. FRAPH, the right-wing Haitian Death Squad organization, was sponsored by the CIA. As soon as the Duvalier dictatorship and the dreaded Tonton Macoutes and their powerful moneyed allies were thrown out and a popular democracy took power (Aristide won, I believe, about 90 percent of the vote), the U.S. stopped all assistance to Haiti and made sure all monies from the International Monetary Fund dried up. So while we were insisting that Afghanistan turn over bin Laden, the U.S. government was refusing to extradite Toto Constant, the head of FRAPH terrorist organization, who'd been indicted for murdering 3,000 civilians in Haiti. Of course, the last thing we wanted was Constant on trial talking about his CIA connections. So he's living a cushy life in the States. No one seemed to notice the contradiction and hypocrisy. If we had a right to invade Afghanistan, surely Haiti had a right to bomb the United States.

The U.S. has opposed democracy and overthrown various democracies—Chile, Iran, Haiti, and Nicaragua come immediately to mind—always while pretending that we're in favor of democracy, that we're champions of democracy. We have underwritten torture regimes and mass-murder regimes, and the American public by and large believes we love democracy and are trying to promote it around the world. Absurd. We are the enemy of progressive forces, of the poor and oppressed all over the world. But you can read 10 American poetry journals without finding a single political poem, a single poem about the horrors of American colonial aggression, just as you can read

10 American newspapers without being told the truth about America's international agenda.

The entire Middle East despises us largely because of our wholesale support for the theft of Palestine and for the "transfer"—the ethnic cleansing—of the Palestinian people that Israel has been undertaking since 1947, by making life so unbearable that the indigenous population has no choice but to leave. Israel is a savage, racist, militaristic government hellbent on stealing what little of the Palestinian homeland they haven't yet already expropriated. But that's still taboo to say out loud in the United States. There was the overthrow of the popular Mosaddegh government in Iran, of course; our destruction and occupation of Iraq; and our general racist disdain for the Arab world. You will find almost nothing about America's role in the world in most contemporary American poetry. There have been three or four anthologies of political poetry published after 9/11 and some readings opposing the war, and that's all honorable and fine. But the mainstream poetry press doesn't want poetry dealing with the horrors of the world, and of America's central role in generating those horrors. Read African, Latin American, Middle Eastern, Asian, and Eastern European poetry, and it's filled with political perception, the devastations of hunger, poverty, war, exploitation, corporate greed. But you'll find little of it in the American mainstream poetry.

Well, the landlords of the world don't write about the oppression of their tenants. The landlord-banking class needs to avoid the subject, go into denial, rationalize, and put its attention elsewhere. Mainstream white American poets, on the whole, seem to know as little about the role of their country in the world as the ordinary, uneducated population. Human beings have a genius for believing what they find convenient to believe. Qabbani says: "What is poetry if it does not declare mutiny?/If it does not topple tyrants. . ." if it does not "dislodge the crown/Worn by the powerful kings of this world." Now, Terry, you're in the minority. You're a Vietnam vet, and one of those who can't help but write about those horrors, so you probably have a similar sense of the poetry community's turning its back on the rest of the world. On the other hand, the poets, or at least some segment of them, are just about the only community of artists in the country who have organized against the horrors of this administration, against the invasions and wars. Against the war crimes. Sam Hamill did a fine job organizing that resistance among poets, and Allen Cohen, Clive Matson, William Heyen, and others who put out political anthologies are to be thanked. Poets like yourself, going around giving politically conscious poetry readings, reminding the audience of the unspeakable horrors of Vietnam, are to be thanked.

TH: The last poet whose name most people would probably recognize (even if they had never read him) was Robert Frost, who even appeared on *The Tonight Show*. The audience at the majority of poetry readings in the U.S. today seems to be mostly other poets. Why do you think this is?

SK: The 20th century was the age of the novel. Dana Gioia insists that the reason poetry was popular in 19th century America was that poems were published as a matter of course in American newspapers. I'm skeptical of his theory. Lots of American newspapers today publish a poem every week, usually in their book-review section. But many of the poems are unintelligible and reinforce the public's perception that poetry is boring. Well, a great deal of it is. Edna Millay (a wonderful, much undervalued poet) was popular during her life, and Robinson Jeffers was until his reputation was destroyed by his opposition to the Second World War. I don't pretend to understand the entire sociology of the thing, but surely the fact that American and British poetry was dominated by poets who were difficult to read helped destroy the potential audience. Eliot, Stevens, and hundreds of utterly opaque, consciously elitist, high-modernist poets—two or three generations of them—made certain that the public would find little of interest in modern poetry, so people stopped reading the stuff.

But the huge spoken-word scene shows that people crave poetry, that poetry is very much alive. And it's fiercely political: rants and shouts about oppression, the kind of thing the university poets just don't have the courage or interest to do. The immense popularity of Rumi in various contemporary translations (I suspect it's a somewhat sexed-up

Rumi) shows that there's an audience. Maybe that curious musical form we call poetry will never again, in this country, find a mass audience. It still has that broad attraction, that mass audience, in parts of South America and Russia. Qabbani's love poetry is known all over the Arab world and Neruda remains an international hero. Robert Pinsky was able to turn himself into a national presence when he became poet laureate. Bob Hass did, too. Hass turned the laureate into a public figure and should be given a lot of credit for that. And Collins, whom I've already yammered about at some length. No, poetry might never become a popular literary form again—though if we return to an aesthetic that includes intelligibility, it might have a shot at it. As an anthologist, I've tried to showcase that sort of poetry. *The Maverick Poets* was the first anthology to showcase America's brilliant accessible poets. From Ginsberg and the Beats to wonderful poets like Al Zolynas, Dorianne Laux, Sharon Olds, Hal Norse, and Charles Bukowski. Charles Webb's recent *Stand Up Poetry* anthology has tried to do that too—I think very successfully. Billy Collins' *Poetry 180* and Milosz's *Luminous Things* and other anthologies I've seen recently are trying to do that, too. There are scores of American poets these days writing brilliantly readable and memorable poems. But most of the better-known journals are publishing stuff that seems dull and obtuse, and the mainstream, large-distribution anthologies—I'm thinking of those old Al Poulin canonical anthologies and the *Best American Poetry* anthologies and the recent J. D. McClatchy anthology of American poetry—are not, by and large, vibrantly readable and engaging. In just about any of the *Best American Poetry* anthologies, you'll find three or four terrific poems, a dozen pretty good ones, and the rest of little or no interest whatsoever. Not that they're poorly made or amateurish or without skill—but they're boring—and usually unintelligible. What sane citizen would want to go out and read more of that stuff? What we need are more first-rate anthologies of poems that the common reader can fall in love with—the "common reader" being a term, by the way, that implies the fine, experienced, sensitive reader, the man or woman in love with good books!

Once the public sees that poetry is readable again, that it's human and touching and insightful and memorable and fun, there might be a shift in the wind and verse might have a shot at becoming a popular art form again. I wish some big-city newspaper or large circulation magazine would hire me to be their poetry editor! I'd do it for free! There are so many wonderful poets writing these days—people who should be read and enjoyed by a large public.

TH: Who have you been reading and why? How does what you read affect your own writing?

SK: In the past week or two, I've read Mary Oliver's new book; Kim Addonizio's feisty new collection, *What Is This Thing Called Love*; and Julia Alvarez's new collection—all three of those books are quite wonderful. I've also been reading some of Kafka's parables because I was teaching them. And a book on the history of Korea by Bruce Cumings. He's our most reliable Koreanologist (okay, so that's not exactly the word I'm looking for). And there's a book I just got out of the library with an essay about the history of Feistinger's cognitive dissonance theory that I want to get to sometime in the next few days. It's an essential concept about human dynamics, how we function and why we go into denial, believe those stupid myths, and refuse to look reality in the face. And this evening I was reading a wonderful book about the real dynamics of the U.N. called *Calling the Shots*, a book about how the U.S. has turned the organization into an instrument of its own foreign policy. I don't read the high-flown poets, the Poundians and esotericoids. Utterly impossible. I know that when I get lost in line two or three it's not because I can't keep up with genius, but because they're either not interested in or not capable of real communication. God save us from the avant-garde!

Ah, but those human poets who are speaking English and have something to say. Julia Alvarez I'd never read before, but for an occasional poem here and there. She's very, very good. Moving and human and authentic. There's a sweetness and a goodness about her that one doesn't find often in contemporary poetry. Very trustworthy—intelligent and vulnerable. She's not protecting anything and she's not trying to impress her reader. In fact, one has to look closely to see her subtlety and prosodic skill. She's really writing a loose blank verse, and every poem in this new collection is 30 lines long, divided into three 10-line stanzas. So she's a formalist! Kim Addonizio loves sonnets and form, too. Terrific craft, and she's always transgressive and provocative and often wonderful.

Mary Oliver is probably the most remarkable poet we have. Now, that is really what spiritual presence means. She's one of those visionaries who has been writing one poem all her life—the formula is as obvious and transparent as possible: she describes some bird or snake or frog or flower, and the world is suddenly luminous and present before her and the reader. And most of her poems are delicious and utterly believable. She has a brilliant ear that almost never errs. And she just, somehow, draws you in and you're hooked. Our most religious, most visionary contemporary. Like Whitman, she doesn't really have to work toward the epiphanic, toward the transcendent, because she's very much there at the poem's beginning. Luminous stuff!

There are, it seems to me, lots and lots of splendid poets writing these days. We need more anthologies like my old *Maverick Poets* and Charles Webb's *Stand Up Poetry* (which you and I are both in)— anthologies that are showcasing altogether readable and engaging poems.

And of course I read lots of news stuff, especially on-line. News services like *Jewish Peace News* and *International Solidarity* and *Gush Shalom*, so I can keep up with what's going on in Occupied Palestine— the latest murders and betrayals and nightmares.

The effect on me of my reading? When a poem is wonderful, I always have the urge to write one just like it! An imitation of that writer's style. Kim Addonizio's voice appeals to me—she's my kind of rebel. I constantly learn from Dorianne Laux. Her work is often breathtaking. But these days I'm trying to write lots of political poetry, and there aren't too many North American models—Ginsberg, an occasional poem here and there. Of course, I spent a couple of years translating Cardenal and a few years translating Neruda's political poetry, so I've been looking at models of that kind of poetry for a long time. Brecht is wonderful at times at that kind of in-your-face, anti-Hitlerian lyrical polemic.

TH: What is your advice to someone who is just beginning to write poetry?

SK: Of course, as I've made clear, I have an agenda—I want poets to do whatever magic they do while honoring their ability to communicate. The cognitive vacuity of post-modern poetry doesn't appeal to me at all, and I would hope that the younger poets writing take their inspiration from those poets—present and past—who had something of use to say, and who wanted to get it said so that the reader would hear it. That means craft at the service of content. "Content" has been something of a dirty word these past many decades. Write as wildly and uninhibitedly as you wish, but make sure you're bringing the reader with you. Otherwise, you're just showing off, just spinning your wheels. But my more general advice would be write as much as you can; read as much as you can; read widely not only in the American tradition and the British tradition, but at the fount of world poetry. One can as easily fall in love with Catullus and Villon as with contemporary American poets. Find the poets you love and imitate them—imitate their tones and gestures and ways of getting into a poem. Don't be afraid that you'll sound like them or end up being imitative! You will simply end up learning new strategies, new ways to shape your own poetry. Fall in love with as many poems and poets as you can. When you find poems you love, xerox them or scan them into your computer and compile an anthology. That way you can keep handy those poems you most relish! And of course, have lots of fun with poetry. That's the real, ultimate motivator. It's a frustrating kind of fun, a hair-pulling-out kind of fun, but mastering anything is difficult and frustrating. The joy of composing, of creating art, is a wonderful kind of joy! Also, study under everyone you can, take as many workshops and sit at the feet of as many poets as you can. Let it all influence you. A point will come when you know what you want out of poetry.

TH: Finally, Steve, as we talked about earlier, most people (at least in the U.S.) don't read poetry. What significance do you think poetry and poets have in the world today?

SK: Terry, a few days ago, a poet/teacher friend of mine, Glory Foster, told me something that Nelson Mandela recently said. She was paraphrasing but it went something like this: "Poetry cannot stop a bullet, but it can bear witness to oppression and cruelty." Yes! Poets— all writers—can bear witness. And I'm not sure poets do this more often or better than do nonfiction writers, memoirists, novelists, essayists, and short story writers. All those crafts aspire to the conditions of poetry just as poetry, on some level, aspires to the conditions of music. Since this dreadful invasion and occupation of Iraq, thousands of poets around the country have been writing poems protesting the war, poems of anguish and dissent, and they've been giving readings (as you well know since, as a Vietnam vet, you've been engaged in anti-war poetry since the 1970s), and making their voices heard. Well, heard as much as poets can be heard above the din of newsspeak and official rhetoric. There have been, as I've already mentioned, several anthologies since 9/11 in which American poets voice their concerns, their sorrow and anger. Sam Hamill, when he began editing his antiwar anthology, already had some 13,000 such poems up on his website.

Yesterday I heard a reading by Adrienne Rich and Robert Creeley at the annual Border Voices festival at San Diego State University. Rich, a highly political, socially conscious poet, began with two poems by Muriel Rukeyser, the first of which was a powerful short poem beginning, "I lived in the first century of world wars." Creeley, interestingly, began his reading with Matthew Arnold's "Dover Beach," a way of letting the audience know that this is not the first time by any means that human tribes have slaughtered each other—those "ignorant armies" that "clash by night," while the poem's narrator tells his beloved that we must remain faithful to one another, now that the sea of Faith is at its ebb! Of course, the idea of the horror of war being an indication of the breakdown of Christianity is rather fanciful, to say the least, since the inter-Christian wars went on for several hundred years and, in fact, the Catholics and Protestants in Ireland are still fighting. But that sense that the values by which the culture lived has ruptured is, indeed, the feeling that such wars engender.

Arnold captures that sense of despair in that marvelous poem, and Creeley, in a discussion later in the day, could only shake his head at the level of hatred in the world, the ease with which we make "enemies" and then go about slaughtering them. That it's the poets who tell those sorts of terrible truths, and that we find the language for our own insights in the words of those poets who came before us, attest to the power of poets to bear witness.

But I had a more moving experience at that fine poetry reading yesterday. Every year when I go to Border Voices I see old friends, and this time I saw my old friend and colleague from San Diego State University, Minas Savvas. Minas was a professor of comparative literature for many years and is a translator of some of the great contemporary Greek poets and a poet in his own right. I remembered, some 21 years ago, when his son was born, a boy who had, as it turned out, a rare congenital illness that did not permit his muscles to develop normally. The first few years had been full of anxiety for Minas and his wife, but things, I take it, had more or less stabilized and had gotten better over the years. Yesterday, Minas and I chatted for several minutes in the rotunda about this and that and then he said to me, "You know, my son died." I was shocked. It had been two years ago. The boy was 19 and had died in his arms. Minas looked out at the grounds around where we were, in Aztec Center, and told me that his boy and he used to walk around that center often. His son loved the bowling alley that was there and had a fondness for that whole part of the campus. Minas said that for the past two years, since his son's death, it had been difficult for him to go there, to Aztec Center, because the pain was too powerful. "He died in my arms," he said to me again. And then he asked me if I remembered the Robert Frost poem "Out, Out" about the young boy killed by the buzz saw. That line about them listening to his heart, "Little? less? nothing!" Minas said to me quietly, "Now I understand what that means. My boy died in my arms. Little? less? nothing!" And that was all my old friend could or wanted or needed to say about it. He'd found the language for the unspeakable grief of that death, his son's final moment, in a poem by Robert Frost.

Okay, just one more thing. I want—by way of answering your question about the significance of poetry, its role in the world—to quote the final lines of a poem about the current Iraq nightmare that was published in one of those recent antiwar anthologies. It's from a very fine anthology put together by Allen Cohen and Clive Matson called *An Eye for An Eye Makes the Whole World Blind*, which I mentioned earlier. It's a poem by a 12-year-old girl named Mariah Erlick. Her poem ends like this:

> Sunday, Dad and I watched T.V.
> We saw the orange jumpsuits of the dead fire-men
> who died that they might restore one thread
> in the lop-sided web of life and failed.
> He said,
> *It is going to be a big religious war.*
> *When I was young it was Vietnam.*
> *Someone should stand up and talk*
> *to say how horrible war is*
> *how terrible hate is.*
> Well, Dad, this is me.
> I'm here.
> I'm talking.

Steve Kowit

A Note Concerning My Military Career

After I'd sent the Army my letter of resignation, two beefy Intelligence types
showed up at my place in the Fillmore with a huge reel-to-reel tape recorder,
& without mincing words I tore into America's despicable agenda:
the circle of hell reserved for our savage carpet-bombing campaign
against the people of Vietnam & the puppet state the U.S. was trying
to force down their throats. Which was why, I explained, I wouldn't put
on their fucking uniform ever again & why, if I had to fight, it would be
for the other side.
        Quiet, courteous, polite, they sat there for two hours
listening to my ferocious rant till I asked what exactly it was they needed
to know, & one of them said they had really been sent to find out if I
was planning to shoot President Johnson, or do something else of that sort,
& I laughed & said no, & we shook hands & they packed up & left.
But a month later, when the Army sent me the transcript to sign & return,
I brought it instead to a young San Francisco attorney whose family firm
did *pro bono* work for resisters, & Josh Callihan read that whole eighteen
page harangue & looked up & told me how much he liked what I'd said,
& when I asked him what to do next, he advised me to get the hell out of town
as fast as I could. Which, I did. I ran for my life & for the lives of all those
they were trying to get me to kill, & of nothing I've done in this world
have I ever been prouder.
        Listen, if you're reading this poem & you're young
or desperate enough to think of enlisting, or have already been suckered in,
understand that despite all those self-righteous fairy-tales about freedom
& peace, this nation has been from its genocidal beginnings addicted
to empire, plunder & perpetual war. Those combat flicks you watched
        as a kid,
& the sanctimonious propaganda that passes for news, & the swaggering,
hawkish prattle puked from the lips of our politicians & pundits—that spew
stinking of corpses & money—are meant to convince young men
& women like you to massacre, city by city & village by village,

America's villain *du jour*, adding, every few years, another small state
that stepped out of line to its necklace of skulls.
& for those of you who will march to your own graves in so doing,
the powers that sent you will bow their heads & present to your folks
the flag that was draped on the box they carted you home in.
                    Friend, find any way that you can to resist
or escape. If you have to run for your life, for chrissake, run for your life.

[Editor's Note: This poem is reprinted from personal email from Kowit
to several friends (July, 2014), and differs slightly from the version
reprinted online.]

Steve Kowit

Israel No Beacon of Democracy, Diversity

The organization Stand With Us has recently put up a billboard in Helena celebrating Israel's diversity, a billboard that attempts to paint a happy face over the ugly reality of that nation's ongoing human rights violations and its fear of real diversity.

But it is also meant to counter that other Helena billboard campaign which urges the United States to stop giving Israel billions of dollars each year in military aid, a campaign to which, as a Jewish American advocate of human rights, I have been proud to contribute.

Surely, Israel's most notable characteristic remains its violent intolerance of diverse cultures, ethnicities, and religions, an insistence that only Jewish citizens can have full human rights in that nation. It is no secret that Jews from anywhere in the world are granted automatic citizenship rights in Israel while non-Jews are given no such rights. Is that how a genuine democracy behaves? Clearly, Israel does not want a multicultural population, does not want diversity: it wants a state in which all or almost all its citizens are Jewish.

Not surprisingly, Israel privileges Jewish citizens over non-Jewish citizens in numerous other ways as well. For example, residents of Jewish towns in Israel now have the right to exclude Arab families from renting apartments or buying homes in those communities. Isn't that precisely the sort of housing discrimination that Jews and African-Americans fought against for decades here in the U.S.? Can one name any other nation on earth that permits such blatant discrimination?

David Ben-Gurion, Israel's founding father and first prime minister, announced as far back as 1937 that he was in favor of "compulsory transfer," what we now call ethnic cleansing, and that Israel could only become a viable Jewish state if no more than 20 percent of its population was non-Jewish. And based on that chilling ideology pre-state Israel confiscated 78 percent of the Palestinian homeland in 1948 through military aggression against a civilian population, dispossessing three-quarters of a million people from their land and forcing them to flee to refugee camps and lives of desperate poverty. The numerous massacres and acts of intimidation that forced those people to flee for their lives are by now thoroughly documented.

But 78 percent of another people's land apparently wasn't enough, so Israel has been illegally gobbling up the West Bank since 1967, despite the fact that the constant confiscation of Palestinian and Bedouin lands by the Israeli state is a continual violation of international law. Right now the Israeli Knesset is finalizing the Prawer-Begin bill which will force 40,000 Palestinian Bedouins off their land in the southern Naqab (Negev) and destroy about 30 villages where those people live.

Progressive Jewish organizations such as Rabbis for Human Rights and Jewish Voice for Peace have joined with other human rights organizations in supporting the UN Special Rapporteur on Adequate Housing and the International Fact-Finding Mission on Israeli Settlements in condemning the compulsory transfer of Palestinians, Israel's continual flouting of international law, and its pervasive violations of human rights. Nonetheless, Israel continues to build illegal settlements in the West Bank, and East Jerusalem continues to be "Judaized," its Christian and Moslem inhabitants being forcibly removed and their homes given to Jewish settlers.

Few Americans know that Israeli Arab towns receive a pittance of what Jewish communities receive for schools and infrastructure, welfare and social services, or that Palestinian Israeli citizens who have married spouses living in the West Bank or Gaza are not allowed to bring their spouses to live with them in Israel. Does a country that practices such brutal forms of discrimination deserve U.S. tax dollars?

Just in the past few weeks the European Union itself has joined the Boycott, Divest and Sanctions (BDS) movement, announcing it will no longer fund or support Israeli business enterprises operating in the illegally occupied territories, businesses that profit from the 46-year occupation of Palestinian land. And every nation in the world except Israel, including even the United States, accepts that the West Bank and Gaza are occupied lands. It's only Israel that claims those lands are "disputed," a term that implies that Israel, ever expansionist, wants to claim ownership of that territory too.

Surely the United States should not be complicit in these outrageous crimes and human rights violations. Which is why Jews of conscience in Israel, the United States, and around the world have for the past several years actively joined forces with others who believe in cultural diversity and social justice to demand that the United States stop giving billions of American tax dollars each year to a country that is anything but the enlightened liberal democracy it pretends to be.

[From "Snapshot"]

At night, a man is sitting at his desk in pain, aging,
full of fears & dreams, till Jesse barges in
& nuzzles his left leg & says, Hey
you know that open box of Milk Bones
in the kitchen? Well, I've been thinking. . .

—from Kowit's book of poems *The First Noble Truth*

Tributes

Deborah Allbritain

Sappho Learns of Your Death

> *. . .even now*
> *when the deer remember,*
> *the grass falls out of their mouths*

> *(an Homage to Steve Kowit)*

All night I pummeled
these silken pillows,
hurled every
ring and bracelet
into the fire—

In the courtyard
still drenched
from April rains,

among the sweet fennel
and sage,
I fell to my knees
just a little short
of dying myself—

And as magnolia blossoms
fell like pale slips
into my lap,
in that unearthly spray
of dawn light,

I thought
I heard your voice,
alive
as the wind,
O my beloved—
Then you were gone.

[Editor's Note: Epigraph is from a poem in Kowit's collection *The Gods of Rapture*. Full text of the poem appears on page 228 of this book.]

Peter Bolland

[A Pillar of Our Own Reach]

Just found out that my friend and poetry mentor Steve Kowit died last night. He was seventy-six. He was a remarkable poet, and his support of my poetry and work as a singer-songwriter meant the world to me. It's one thing when a fan says, "great job," but when a writer of Steve's caliber goes out of his way to talk about how powerful your work is, it stops you in your tracks and emboldens you to do more, go further, and slip deeper.

Steve Kowit changed my life. I took his poetry class at Southwestern College three fall semesters in a row a couple years back. After a long day of teaching my own classes, I'd relish the opportunity to sit in his class one evening a week and share poems with a group of committed and serious writers under the loving guidance of the master. And that's another thing. Not only was he a world-class poet and an expert in the form, he was flat out a master teacher. I learned a lot about how to relax and be myself in the classroom from him. He never pretended to be anything other than what he was—he knew it was enough.

Steve, I love you and carry you with me in all of my work. You shaped so many—there are hordes of us writers out here who count you as a pillar of our own reach. (He probably would have hated that last sentence and would have gently but insistently suggested that I cut it). Here is one of his beautiful poems from the book *Lurid Confessions,* a collection published when he was in his forties: "Crossing the River." [The poem is reprinted on page 70 of this book.]

Duff Brenna

Something about Steve

Sui generis—one of a kind, unique, in a class of his own—defines the
poet under consideration today. Steve Kowit. . .because, well, that was
what we called him. But the *trouble-free* pronunciation of those three
syllables belies the multi-dimensional figure they describe.

Trouble-free? Not a bit. Kowit was demanding when it came to his
views about poetry, art of any kind, political beliefs, the rights of
animals—vegetarian diets versus carnivore-omnivore-raptor-
predators specific to the human species. Serious subjects for a man
who was an idealistic, over-awed lover of nature as well—its
profundities, its depthless wonder, its staggering beauty that brought
forth lines such as:

A minnow
that had sloshed out of someone's bait bucket,
& that I came within an inch of stepping on,
convulsed in agony.
Delighted to assist,
I tossed it back into its ocean:
Swirling eddies sucked about the rocks,
[. . .]
& the sun sank pendulously
over the Pacific shelf.
[. . .]
all the hills of Ocean Beach
glowing
in the rouged light
of midwinter sunset.
Even now
it pleases me to think
that somewhere

in the western coastal waters off America
that minnow is still swimming.

  —from "Joy to the Fishes" in *Lurid Confessions*

Kowit was all that I've mentioned above, but he was convulsively funny as well. He had a quirky, sometimes absurd hilarity, neither jaded nor cruel—more Freudian if one could say Freud had a sense of humor:

A Swell Idea

One of these days
while demonstrating the use
of the possessive pronoun
preceding the gerund
I'll tell her a little joke,
grow playful,
stroke the soft hairs
on the back of Melanie's neck,
then slip my hand
over her breast.
Just as I've dreamed!
She'll groan.
She'll giggle & put
her hand over mine.
She'll love it!
If not, what have I lost?
If she screams
& the others rush in
I'll deny everything.
I'll stand there
shaking my head,
"She's crazy she's
making it up she
practically forced me
for chrissake I'm

sick I'm a sick man
I need help
Help me!"
I'll cry out
in a hoarse,
broken voice
& slip to my knees
& bury my face in my hands

  —from *Lurid Confessions*

In my youth I found out that if you wanted to get girls interested, it was very helpful if you made them laugh. I had memorized so many jokes, soft and semi-porn, that I could go on for an hour, get her giggling then laughing out loud.

When I was courting my significant other, many years ago now, I used Steve Kowit on her. I pulled out his *Lurid Confessions* and had her laughing until she was helpless. I've used *Lurid Confessions* on friends and visitors whenever it seemed to be needed to enliven the evening. He always works.

We grieve you, but damn it, Steve, it's got to be said: you're dead, but you still have the power to make us think deeply about the world we live in and, perhaps most important of all, you bring us together with joy and laughter.

Thank you, my friend of forty years.

Tim Calaway

The Poetry Teacher

For Steve Kowit

He told you the secret to poetry,
which was really quite simple:
Tell a story, and tell it well.
Find your way to say it
in simple language
that anyone could understand.
I'll miss his crooked grin,
his curls ruffled and askew,
the way he hitched his suspenders
while listening with fading ears
to our earnest attempts
to impress him.
The way he would nod
and say, "Good, now rewrite
it a dozen times and
you might have something."
I will miss that.

Brandon Cesmat

Dinners To-Go

For Steve Kowit

First, I read "Last Will" aloud, then
halfway through "Notice," I heard
loud voices upstairs so I set down the glass of whiskey
poured to mourn the passing of Steve Kowit and
went to see what was the matter.

Steve would've made the interruption into a poem,
a funny one. Something like "Carpe Interruptus" with
an opening line about how the moment seizes us,
jealous as hell of all other moments,
their winking possibilities strutting by.

It's true, diems don't hang out on street corners,
waiting for our come-on.
They run by and don't care if we can keep up.
So we can run the other way, high-fiving as many as traffic allows,
or we can find our vantage points—carpe locale—and
trade knucks as the parade passes because
all our moments are looking for us;
they'll find us in the desert, feeding apple to a coyote or
lying on low tide's hard-packed sand so we can stretch our backs.
In San Diego's Gaslamp, Steve ordered three dinners to-go because
"we might need them" on our walk across downtown
where, sure enough, the homeless, more visible than accessible poems,
found us. People, coyotes, moments, poems.

Blossoms interrupted, so many rosebuds gathered
and gone to waste, Steve might say, unless

their dropping petals gather our notice,
moment after moment in this seasonal strip tease.

Rebecca Chamaa

The Most Meaningful Memorial

Leave it to a group of poets to create the best memorial (celebration of life) I have ever attended. The last funeral I went to I got the giggles so badly, because the whole thing seemed so absurd. A pastor who barely knew the deceased read off a list of things he had been told by her family. There was nothing connecting me to the memory of the person I once knew.

But yesterday was different. Way different.

I wrote two weeks ago that my mentor, teacher, and friend Steve Kowit had unexpectedly died.

Yesterday a group of his students, which I have been studying poetry with for two years, gathered in the home of one of our fellow students. We sat around in a circle in the living room. There was coffee, homemade brownies, a variety of nuts, and bottled water.

We talked about our future as a group. We talked about how to proceed without our beloved Steve. We decided to meet as before, on the last Sunday of the month, and work our way through a poetry workshop book that Steve wrote, *In the Palm of Your Hand*. We decided to take turns facilitating the group. We all agreed no one could step into the shoes of Steve.

After we had taken care of business, we started talking about personal things. It happened naturally. One person told a story about Steve, about the suspenders he always wore, about how he would ask us to raise our hands if we didn't understand the poem we just heard, about how he used to force snacks on us.

The stories continued. People brought out poems and we went around the circle, and most people read a poem or two that they had written about him since his passing. I cried so hard, that tissues were handed to me from every direction. Most people cried. I found it hardest to keep my tears under control when the men cried. All of our hearts were breaking.

Then someone would say something else and we would laugh, from the deepest parts of ourselves.

We sat that way for three hours, telling stories about "Our Steve," about a man who had made such an impact in all of our lives. We laughed and cried together. We shared our grief, our heartache, our sorrow. We shared our incredible loss. We shared our love.

And we bonded. We healed. We found a way to go on, a way that would have made Steve happy. In fact, the whole gathering would have made him happy. We talked about the man. The real man, as we all knew him and loved him.

We honored his memory in our togetherness, in our laughter, and in our tears.

Leave it to a group of poets to make me feel every high and every low for three straight hours and want to see them all again as soon as possible, because they hold the magic of memory and healing in their words.

It's not good-bye. We will still have his words to guide us. And maybe we will even leave the chair at the head of the table open, so he can join us as we critique our art in the way he taught us, with laughter and love.

Rebecca Chamaa

The Last Act: Steve Kowit

I can't open my e-mails. I need to clean out my inbox, but I can't see his words right now. He died yesterday. I loved him.

His poetry group was the first place where I openly came out about my schizophrenia. Even with that, he once told me I was one of the clearest thinkers he knew.

He never judged me. He never treated me as less than. He was a champion of my poetry and prose. He wrote me a letter for graduate school. I got accepted.

When graduate school turned out to be a joke, he felt personally responsible for encouraging me to try the program. Of course, the problem with the program had nothing to do with him. I applied to another school. He wrote another letter. I got accepted.

He published my poems in *Serving House Journal,* and accepted a poem for *The Reader* that was supposed to come out this month. I don't know if it ever will. I wish it would, so I could hold on to the memory that he believed in me. [1]

That's it. He was a successful writer, and teacher, and he believed in me.

Of course, he believed in hundreds and hundreds of people, but all of us felt as if we were the only one. He had that knack. He possessed the ability to make every writer (most of all, poets) he encountered feel as if they were special, and he gave all of us his attention.

He wrote countless letters, and endorsements, and gave feedback continuously on the poems that flooded his inbox. I don't think he believed in God, but I believe enough for both of us, and if there is an inbox in heaven, his is already full of poems from all his poetry friends he told me went before him. He is reading poetry. I am sure of it.

And making jokes, and serving snacks to everyone, "Here, try one of these. Have some. Take some home."

Home, he is home now, or at least that is what people say. I thought his home was with us. He was always a natural wherever he was. Laughing. Joking. Laughing. Joking. He freely gave out good, sound writing advice, all kinds of advice on how to live, and be a writer.

He wanted us all to succeed, and the funny thing is he made us all feel like we had.

I had no confidence as a writer when I met him. I wouldn't even call myself that. I was just someone who wrote an occasional poem. He built me up, block by block. I have a business card now that has the word, writer, printed on it.

He gave me that, and so much more.

Good-bye, my friend, my mentor. I have to keep pushing on, because that is how you would have wanted it. "Do it!" "Go for it!" "That's a great idea!" "You are so smart!"

Your words will now have to hold me over until we meet at the next poetry workshop, the one where you'll need to introduce me all over again.

You are among the greats now.

[¹ Editor's Note: As Ms. Chamaa wrote five days later in her blog:

My mentor sent this in for publication just before he died. I can't tell you how much it means to me to see it on the Internet and in print this morning. Thank you, Steve. You continue to be good to me.

On the 8th of April, *The Reader* ran the poem "Tying the Knot" with a footnote from Steve:

Rebecca Chamaa's poem is an intriguing model of the "list poem," and a clever poem about failed love.]

Anna DiMartino

A Cricket's Prayer

> Dying cricket
> How he sings out
> his life.
>
> —Basho

My daughter hates them,
the crickets that have colonized
my kitchen since summer,
the crescendo of their chorus
at night. She begs me to kill them.
I tell her to be brave.

But while she sleeps, I tiptoe
through the dark kitchen,
a flashlight in one hand,
a slipper in the other,
and one by one, I slay them.

When I was her age, 15,
I spent a summer in Colorado.
I remember putting on a sock,
feeling the tickle of a cricket in the toe.
Thirty years later and I still shake
out my socks. I've never told her.

Last night, I massacred six, swept
their broken bodies and severed legs,
antennae still twitching,
into the plastic dustpan.

And then I saw one swimming
in the dog's water bowl and thought

of Steve Kowit's "Prayer," the tip
of his finger lifting midges and gnats
from his dog's water bowl, and suddenly,
I wanted to save this one,
wanted to hear it sing.

Clyde Fixmer

Dear Mary

I was shocked to hear of Steve's death . . . I had hoped to have him as a friend for many more years.

Steve was the first person I met when I came to teach at SDSU 36 years ago. He introduced me to other poets and writers in the area and arranged for me to do a reading. We had several friends and acquaintances in the larger poetry community around the country as well, and shared a love of good writing, especially the satirical kind.

He and I also cared very deeply about the plight of the disenfranchised, especially the Palestinians. As you know, Steve was a tireless advocate for them and their cause, and his support will be sorely missed.

I love Steve's writing. He was one of the most imaginative poets I've ever read, and we shared a belief that writing should be clear and accessible to everyone. His writings are characterized by meaningful topics expressed in language that is free from the faults of most of his contemporaries, especially those who specialize in colorless imagery and dullness of ideas and style.

It's a shame that Steve's writings have not yet garnered the recognition he deserves. I believe his time will come—and whether it be soon or slow, it will be so.

I am grieved that I have lost a wonderful pal and an irreplaceable colleague, and that you have lost your husband and best friend.

Yours,
Clyde Fixmer

Bill Harding

[A Genuine Treasure]

The most generous artist in San Diego is dead—poet Steve Kowit. His poetry was music, the deliberately discordant minor tones jarring with the full-bodied brightness of the major keys: our own Thelonious Monk, by way of Brooklyn and all the bumps between there and here. I loved his wit, his outlandish sense of humor, his keen mind, those halting pauses when he read his poems, the way you could hear the smile in his voice. So many of us loved him as friend, mentor, and teacher, and it took him all but the last two years of his life to learn to say "no" to requests. Still, I don't think he ever let any of us down. He showed up, always. He has long been an emblem of what the best of us looks like, and he will remain that for me. We've lost a genuine treasure.

Terry Hertzler

The Golden Years

In Memory of Steve Kowit, April 2015

My toes are numb most of the time now, nerve damage,
side effect of diabetes, part of a litany of age-related issues:

hypertension, congestive heart failure, the list goes on.
I retired last year, but can't survive on Social Security,

teach part-time at the local university. On good days
I still enjoy teaching. But some days it's almost too much.

My mother died more than a year ago, my best friend
from college five years before, father six years earlier,

his younger brother this past July—friends and relatives
are disappearing. I remember sitting alone with my mother

that last hour in the hospice, her breathing almost a panting,
gradually slowing until it stopped altogether. A few weeks

prior, my brother had flown in from Ohio. On her last
clear day we sat in her room, one on either side of her bed.

She looked at me, then at Clark, smiled a small, almost
private smile and said, "Both of my boys are here."

I haven't spoken to my ex-wife in 20 years. Occasionally,
I Google her. She's living in Seattle, teaching

at a community college. *Rebecca.* I'm still writing
about Vietnam, 45 years later. It's never far away.

Life is odd. There's a large ant colony beside
the barrel cactus in my front yard, a spray of fine dirt,

like a private beach, fanning out from the cactus.
Earlier today I was squatting next to it, watching

the always busy ants, when a neighbor walked by, said,
"You should do something about those ants. They'll get

in your house." I considered that idea for a while, pictured
me pouring gasoline, waiting as it slithered its way through

tunnels and crevices, then lighting it up, watching flames
burn it all away. I probably won't do it. Seen enough fires

in my life. When I finally stood up, my knees popped,
creaking like the doors of a long-abandoned car.

I watched the anthill a moment longer, then glanced
at the sky. After thunderstorms most of the day—sky

dull gray or black—the sunset was transformational.
I walked out onto the street, slowly turning in circles,

staring at the shifting colors, the multiplicity of shapes
and textures that made me want to reach up and caress

the clouds, and I continued turning and turning,
head tilted, trying to absorb it all, almost dizzy with joy

and astonishment. But the sky faded, colors bleeding
away, and in the end I felt only sorrow. One of my oldest

friends died yesterday. A week ago he was taken to
the emergency room, two stents placed in his coronary

arteries. But he never really recovered, died in his sleep.
This evening I sat with a half-dozen of his books on my lap,

rereading his poetry, "[A]stonished again / at the unbelievable
colors, / the utter profusion of forms, / the sharp edges

everything has in this world." And I remembered a poem
of mine he particularly liked, "Spring Evening After Rain":

Clouds in the south this evening slant like a long bridge
turning red, then gray, as if fire were the answer to some

unspoken question suggested by the sun. After 45 years,
I'm still surprised. And in my shoulders I feel again the ache

of rucksack & armor, watch starlings settle into pepper trees,
shrug off the long day.

Jackleen Holton Hookway

The Poetry Lesson

For Steve Kowit, June 30, 1938–April 2, 2015

Steal a line from a great poem
because the best poets don't pay
Homage—that word like the godly He,
spelled with a capital H—they take
as if the whole world was their smorgasbord.
Yes, that's what it felt like on that day we hiked
in the Cuyamacas, and all of nature
seemed to be slyly winking
as it sent us bluebird after bluebird, wild
turkey, deer, and that wounded lizard
we found on the path, the one you gently
moved aside with a stick as you swore
to the squeamish among us that its torn-off tail
would regenerate itself in a week. Our group
was mostly poetry students, and you, winking back,
as if you had summoned the gods, arranged
for a lesson so perfect it would be impossible not to write
a poem. So this is mine, the one I'm trying to shape
from your teachings, the day after learning you've gone,
your books spread out over my cluttered desk.
That's another one of your tricks: include in your poem
a reference to the writing of it, like a camera
pulling back to reveal the soundstage, gaffers,
boom mikes and floodlights. After the hike,
a few of us drove to a small lake where your friend Jack
set up a telescope, and we waited to catch
a glimpse of the fledgling eaglet
whose parents had forged a temporary
nest in the brambles. Here's what I remember:
my stomach rumbling as we took turns gazing
into the eyepiece. I wasn't thinking of eaglets,

but Julian apple pie. I was going to have mine *à la mode*
with Dutch crumble crust. (Notice how I've used
assonance and consonance, the mimicking sounds
of brambles/rumbling/crumble/crust?)
But when that large nest rustled, and the fledgling
rose, its new wings flapping, and landed, briefly
on a branch, I forgot about everything
I planned to do later: have lunch
at that roadside café where we always ended up,
the lively political discussion that would ensue,
even the exquisite dessert, its perfect blending
of hot and cold. But then, just as quickly
as it had appeared, the little eagle
dropped back into its nest, out of sight.
Would this be a good place to address
the reader, to instruct?
Listen! When the beauty of a thing insists
on being seen, you must give yourself over
to it, for this is the shimmering everything: the moment
and its volumes of unwritten poems.
But here's the part where I make my confession:
I lied. I never saw that eaglet.
The stupid guy I was dating left his backpack
at the trailhead. And I, being even stupider,
drove him back instead of letting him take my car,
going with you and Jack to see the bird.
But everything else is true: the lizard,
the café where you told us of your miraculous
sighting, the steaming apple pie. I saw you last month
at a workshop you taught. It never occurred to me,
not for a second, that it would be the last time.
You said, *Here's a trick, a really cheap trick:*
End your poem with a rhyme.

Commentary by Hookway on "The Poetry Lesson"

This poem is for my first poetry teacher, Steve Kowit, who passed away on April 2nd. He was a great poet, mentor, and one of the most generous people I've ever met. Steve had several "tricks" for writing poems, which he used in his own work, and I have tried my best to include in this tribute piece. My favorite is this: Tell at least one lie in your poem.

[Editor's Note: Poem and commentary were first published in "Poets Respond," *Rattle* (5 April 2015).]

Thomas E. Kennedy

The Stand-Up Poet

Duff Brenna introduced me to Steve Kowit fifteen or twenty years ago, and he confided in me, prior to introducing him, "Tell me if you don't think Steve looks like Dylan Thomas!"

He did—not only because of the mop of curls on his head, but also because he *looked* like a poet: The way he had of providing, with his face, an amused-sympathetic mirror of whomever he was looking upon.

At least that was how I saw his face. He seemed to *see* you with simultaneous sympathy and amusement, and it wasn't amusement *at* you, it was amusement *with* you; his expression seemed to ask the question: *Isn't it a fine pickle we're in, life, in every sense of the word's meaning—fine?*

He was a *simpatico* guy, and I liked him instantly, and I never stopped liking him or admiring his poems. He was a stand-up poet—as was titled one of the anthologies he was in or edited—and a stand-up guy.

I never saw Steve enough—only a couple or three times in the years I knew him—but we were often in touch in writing, and he never failed to respond positively with a poem and/or an essay to one of my invitations to contribute to an anthology—most of them collaborations with Walter Cummins—despite the fact that we never paid him other than in copies.

And he often read work by me that appeared here and there and consistently dropped me a word of confidence and support for some of the most important pieces to me—I think specifically of a friend about whom I'd written who died much too soon. . . . He seemed always to know.

It seems awful to refer to Steve in past tense—though, of course, we will all be there, some sooner than others.

Meanwhile, let me give a Danish cheer from the bottom of my heart to Steve, his stand-up person and his stand-up poetry—three shorts and a long:

Steve Kowit—let his poetry and his memory live long:
HRA !
HRA !
HRA !
Hraaaaaaaaaaaaaaaa. . .

Ron Koertge

[Bringing the House Down]

A few years ago, the Pasadena Public Library sponsored a series featuring California poets. The interesting thing about that gig was this: California poets were solicited to read other California poets' work. So someone did Bukowski, someone did Jeffers, then Soto, and Levine, and so forth.

I was asked to read some Kowit poems. I loved Steve; we'd been friends for nearly fifty years. I said that it would be a pleasure.

And it was. I talked about Steve's many passions and read "Refugees, Late Summer Night." I dipped in and out of *The Dumbbell Nebula, The First Noble Truth,* and *The Gods of Rapture.* And I read as Steve might have—amorous and ebullient.

There is a poem from *Heart in Utter Confusion* that begins "Because she has been running through a summer downpour." To me, that one always seemed to be the seed for a longer, personal poem called "The Blue Dress," where his wife Mary saves a gopher from one of their many cats, then runs out in the rain to find a safe place for him. It's one of my favorites—passionate, tender, large-hearted. It pretty much brought the house down.

For upwards of twenty minutes, the audience laughed after the funny poems, licked their lips after the sexy ones, and if they cried, they did it softly so as not to miss a word.

Sylvia Levinson

My Steve Kowit

For days, since learning of Steve's death, I have read the emails and Facebook posts from so many whose lives he touched. I have talked with others—heard the words—generous, kind, funny, loving, poet, teacher, mentor, publisher, friend. He was all of those things, had such an impact on hundreds of students, colleagues, friends. He connected me to so many of you beautiful, gifted poets, writers, friends.

And, yes, when I tell of him, I use those words, too. This is how I knew him.

Steve was my first poetry teacher more than 20 years ago and has been over and over again, at workshops, classes, and readings; at The Writing Center, Southwestern College, San Diego Writers Ink; at coffee shops and bookstores and churches. He once asked me to co-teach a class for Seniors and Alzheimer's patients at St. Paul's Villa. What a thrill and validation!

His greeting, always, "How are ya? Ya doin' OK?" in a way that I knew he meant it, he really wanted to know. As we aged together (we are the same age), we began to share news of a bad back or tweaky knees, hearing aids and cataract surgery; how things that used to be easy now took much more energy. Not complaints, but a common bond.

I have not been able to make sense of the reality of his death until today—four days since I heard the impossible news. It left me reeling, shocked, devastated—dramatic words I rarely use, certainly never frivolously or cheaply, their meaning so profound.

It has been impossible to conceive of my world, our world, without him in it. Today I write it, think I can wrap my brain and heart around the truth of it. I don't claim to have been as close to him or known him as well as many. I do not negate others' perhaps even greater feelings of loss. Mine is deep; it is my own. Today I add a word to the list of praise for this man who means so much to me—authentic—he was the most real person I know—an authentic human being. Oh, yes, I'll also add "cheerleader." He always wanted us to do well!

I send to all who loved him, and to his beautiful wife Mary, whom he loved so much and whose loss must be the greatest of all, the wishes, the words he emailed me on my birthday. "Hope it's a wonderful, fertile, productive, healthy deliciously happy year! Hugs & more hugs, love & more love, Steve."

Yours in grief and gratitude,
Sylvia Levinson

Jack Marshall

Steve Kowit

Steve was my oldest friend and toughest critic, longer than most marriages, and at times as hard to sustain. He had little tolerance for ambiguity, especially in poetry, philosophy, politics. He was a soldier in the wars of clarity against obfuscation.

Though a pacifist, Steve could get really angry in defense of some unwritten moral law which had been broken, and against some defenseless creature.

A good description of Steve would be Nietzsche's "having the optimism of a desperado." As a kid, his hair had been matted curls, uncombed, like the original Dylan in a young photo, full head turned toward camera, cupping his hands lighting a cigarette.

The impact of hearing of his sudden death in a call by a mutual friend was immediate, instant severing, pitiless and absolute. It is unlike the mass death in the news we take in without the full weight of specific loss and gravity we feel when someone close to us dies.

Re-reading Steve's poems again, I felt as if I was just beginning to know the extent and depth of the human and animal causes which concerned him, and he gave himself to, like his passion for teaching, his activism for animal rights, his volunteering at a local soup kitchen for the homeless. I could see him active in a larger perspective, in the lives of people outside our friendship; and friendship meant a lot to Steve. He'd keep current, lately mostly about each of our medical conditions, his bad back, my bad eyes. Once, he said we didn't need to ask how each other felt: just exchange our latest medical reports.

And then there was the ancient prophetic wail: "We are a failed species," he'd say when we spoke on the phone, or saw each other, yet his compassion and devotion to protecting animals were boundless, as was his fierce indignation about our wars in Vietnam, Iraq, South America, our country's complicity in Israel's treatment of Palestinians.

A failed species. . .yet his poems express the opposite: some politically outraged, others loving and cherishing his wife Mary, his friends, students, strays, cats and dogs, natural landscapes he would hike and camp on, Central American countries he had traveled in after evading call-up for service in Vietnam.

I learned that he'd become a strict vegetarian. Once, when he was offered a chicken sandwich, he said, "I do not eat sentient beings." The preciseness of "sentient beings" rather than, say, "creatures," drew for me an awareness of other conscious, mindful, life-perceiving existences with feelings, as real as our own, and this openness to life-forms, like his model, Whitman, fills his work.

Driving past a slaughterhouse in the distance from which a sickening smell of butchery filled the air, with a panged look contrasting with his usual high positive energy, Steve lowered his voice to say that cows herded into pens rub each other with nose-kisses, knowing they're on their way to slaughter.

I'm sure Steve must have felt greater agony the more he learned of the many needlessly cruel ways animals were experimented on for the enhancement of a better eye-blush or skin toner.

Another time, when about to visit him and Mary in their home near the Mexican border, I remembered his vehemence on the subject of animal protection, and asked if he would be offended if I wore a leather jacket, it being winter where I lived in San Francisco. "Only if it's still on the animal's back," he said. Thank God, I thought, not a fundamentalist!

Oh yeah, and he was an atheist who'd say "God willing" when wishing you and himself good health. More than a figure of speech, I think it might have been a pod of a prayer to a God he didn't believe in, and if He did exist, Steve said, he'd be against.

In his poetry and essays, as well as his dealings with people, I think of Steve as living and putting into practice the most radical use of language: straightforwardness.

Bill Mohr

Steve Kowit (1938–2015)

Laurel Ann Bogen called me this evening and said that San Diego-based poet Steve Kowit has died. The last time I saw Steve was at the Long Beach Poetry Festival in 2011, at which he was the featured reader in the evening program. The festival was in a gallery space on Atlantic Blvd., the kind of venue that Steve was most comfortable in. He did not read any new poems, but the old ones seemed as lively as ever. Kowit was a performer who knew how to convey that his themes were chosen out of profound necessity. One could see how he might have made a very interesting character actor, but for one drawback. He was far too literate to remove himself from a life devoted to the written word and too blunt to tolerate those who had no such need.

As editor of *The Maverick Poets,* an anthology that included several of the poets who came to be associated with the Stand Up School, Kowit showed that it was possible to integrate non-academic West Coast poetry with the work being done elsewhere in the country. Furthermore, he was one of the few editors I have ever met who had more than a partial grasp of the common poetics that linked those working in Southern California with those based in Northern California. He cared about the poem, not the poet's reputation. He spoke up for poets, such as Kim Addonizio, long before they had achieved their current popularity. His ability to appreciate the poets living in Northern and Southern California may well be an outgrowth of the time he spent as a young poet in San Francisco, when he was a graduate student at San Francisco State, before moving to San Diego.

Kowit was that rare cultural worker, an individual who could truly appreciate the work of others without worrying unduly about whether others appreciated his work. In part, his confidence in his poems came from years of giving poetry readings in which he didn't have to wonder afterwards about the sincerity of the audience's pleasure. It's fashionable to mock sincerity as a virtue worth retaining in a postmodern culture; Kowit mocked the self-indulgent, whether they were poets who read too long or simply people unable to savor the transitory privilege of playfulness. His sincerity had the genius of never seeming didactic. His poems taught you to laugh at yourself. "I died & went to hell & it was nothing like L.A." begins one of his poems. For those of us who live here, the poem is worth posting on the door of one's workroom.

Along with many other poets, I will miss his ever-fermenting amusement at the foolishness of contemporary civilization. We've been given a paradise to celebrate the possession of consciousness within and we cannot resist the temptation to despoil it. Steve, may you rest well on the long journey home, and reemerge in an enduring garden of the ever-ripening.

Bill Mohr

Steve Kowit Post-Script:
Walt Whitman's Butterfly

That singular flight of felicitous whimsy...

Before I headed off to the Los Angeles Times Festival of Books at the University of Southern California, I spent a few minutes working on my bookshelves at home. I have enough new books that I simply must prune (de-accession?) the shelves! Sorting and re-shelving, I found that treasured gifts from other poets awaited me, especially a broadside from Steve Kowit entitled "A Whitman Portrait." It's a 54-line poem with a delicious sense of humor. Kowit loved to let others hoist themselves on their own petard, which in this case is their presumptuousness that the butterfly poised on Whitman's finger in a photographic portrait taken of him in Camden in 1883 was "nothing but papier mâché." Kowit's poem is the pleasure of community formation at its best. Sure, it's an "us against them" poem, but those who have mocked the alleged artificiality of this portrait (with the implied contempt for Whitman's *sentimentality*) deserve this rebuke, which also rebounds to us for the ultimate fate of this species. According to Kowit,

> ...high-resolution spectro-
> analysis proved what any fool could have guessed:
> she was just what she seemed, mortal & breathing,
> a carbon-molecular creature like us: *Papilio*
> *aristodemus*, now all but extinct...

Kowit's critique of contemporary poetry is already blunt and merciless. He was a poet whose eyes partook of "that singular flight of felicitous whimsy," but it must also be said that he saw no reason to spare the feelings of the Great Pretenders.

If it's true there exist fake butterflies
cut out of paper & wire, my guess is
they belong to a later generation of poets.

I'll leave you to figure out the ones who dedicate their lines to fake butterflies, but I don't think such a project deserves more than a few minutes. Better to give yourself the pleasure of the company of Steve Kowit's poems, which are more than willing to alight on your fingertips.

My retrospective thanks again to Steve, for sending me a signed copy of this broadside, dated 12-22-89. I think that may have been the year when Christmas looked fairly bleak. I was living with my first wife, Cathay, in our apartment on Hill Street in Ocean Park and my job as a typesetter did not pay very much. I remember that we probably had about $50 in our bank account on December 22, just enough to buy some basic groceries to get us through the month. We had not bought any Christmas gifts for each other, even tiny ones. I remember standing at the bottom of the staircase and starting to sort through a pile of old mail and assorted loose paper. I saw an envelope from a co-worker at Radio & Records for whom I had done some free-lance work, and I was one hundred percent certain that I had already opened it, but I took another look regardless and there was a simple sheet of paper in it with a notation of hours of work done and a check for well over $200. I couldn't believe it. I suppose that moment was a holiday butterfly. Recollections of many holidays are a blur, but in that instance I still remember how the original expectations for the year's final week made the outcome all the sweeter. I keep thinking at the present moment that there is some meaning I am missing about how one remembers eating well and having a small tree and a few gifts. Is it just nostalgia betraying me, another "bittersweet kaleidoscope"?

[Editor's Note: "A Whitman Portrait" is on page 212 of this book.]

Lynda Riese

His First Day in Heaven

In memoriam Steve Kowit

He refuses to wear the white robe
so carefully measured to fit;

insists on his frayed flannel shirt
and worn jeans torn at the crotch

held up by well-loved suspenders.
He demurs when they offer him wings,

choosing his own two feet;
declines to join the celestial choir

preferring political rants, and good jokes,
his laughter so loud and lusty

that heaven's ethereal ceiling falls in,
waking the dead.

They sit at his feet beguiled,
he in his favorite overstuffed chair,

short legs crossed right over left
as he wished,

lively eyes blue as spring lupine,
his mouth blooming poems.

Lynda Riese

Like Wings

In memoriam Steve Kowit

What shall I do with this poem,
damp as a newborn,

now that you've left us?
It's lonely on the page,

so small, lost
in a sea of blank space

where you had been.
Its lines quiver,

flutter like wings
and fly off to find you

where you sit in a far field
under a shady oak.

They land in your lap,
on your shoulders,

you, St. Francis of words.

R. A. Rycraft

Don't Laugh at My Poetry!

It's heartbreaking. To lose a master poet, certainly. To lose a cherished friend, more so. Steve Kowit no longer walks among us, but he is immortalized in his work. We have that. We can enjoy his wit and hear his voice, feel his passion. . . his compassion. . . sense the shifts in humor through his tone, view our world through the light and lens of his imagery. We—the collective We—have that.

I'm distressed to discover that I took him for granted. Time and distance dull incentive and motivation to keep in touch with someone who should *always be there.* A ruthless email inbox cleaner, I discovered last night that I didn't save a single personal note from Steve. Desperately, I searched all of my email folders and came up empty-handed. You know what I saved? The business notes. Notes filled with details of his upcoming readings at the college where I teach. Notes that strategized his visits to my creative writing classes to discuss his poetry with my students. Notes about essays he wanted me to consider for SHJ. Notes that are perfunctory and to the point. . .well, as perfunctory and to the point as Steve was capable of being, like this note about his fee for reading at the college:

> Ricki—as long as you pay me my minimum fee of $26,000 it will be okay. I know that as soon as I go public with the photos of my sizzling affair with Tiger Woods (yes, he swings both ways), my asking fee will more than triple. So you're getting in under the wire!

And even though I can hear his voice in those notes, most of them lack the easy back and forth banter and teasing I'd find in Steve's personal notes to me—sweet notes between friends talking about Blackwater in Steve's backyard and his animals and my animals and retirement and health and. . . and. . . and. . . and. . . I can't remember what all else. There are none of the notes that included funny or touching animal videos we'd share with one another, the first one being the "Christian the Lion" video which made both of us cry:

https://www.youtube.com/watch?v=Sju3kSTAzdI

I'm heartbroken those emails are gone, that I didn't take care of them, that they are lost through thoughtless acts of efficiency. . .deleting nonessential emails. How could I do that? How could I choose to hang on to all of the notes related to business and toss those precious notes written just for me?

So, this morning I went to our "Friends" bookcase in the entryway of our home and gathered every single Steve Kowit book we own (which is all of them), knowing I would find personal notes inscribed for Duff and for me, remembering—as I picked out *In the Palm of Your Hand, The Maverick Poets, Lurid Confessions, The Dumbbell Nebula, The First Noble Truth, The Gods of Rapture, Greatest Hits 1978–2003, Crossing Borders,* and *Everything is Okay*—Steve sitting at our dining room table, with Duff and friend Clyde Fixmer, after his last reading at the college, eating Eggplant Parmesan and inscribing the stack of books for us with notes like:

> Can I buy this book back from you? I know it's worth lots of money!! ;-)
>
> (In an Uncorrected Proof of *In the Palm of Your Hand*)

AND

> I don't want you guys laughing at my poetry! Hugs & Kisses!!! Steve
>
> (In *Lurid Confessions*)

Ron Salisbury

A Tribute

This text was delivered on 26 April 2015 at an Open Mic
Poetry Reading sponsored by San Diego Writers Ink,
honoring the life of Steve Kowit.

I met Steve thirty-six years ago when I moved to San Diego for the first time. But within the last year, comparing our early poetry years and time in New York City, we discovered that we may have been close to first meeting years before. I was in my late teens, from a farm in Maine; Steve, in his early twenties, had grown up in New York City. There was a coffee house in the East Village called *Les Deux Megots* that had poetry readings every week; this was probably 1962. I got up the courage to read a poem for the first time in public. In the middle of the reading that evening, a guy named Taylor Mead read a letter he had received from Allan Ginsberg who was in India. It was a pages-long letter and Allan talked about bathing in the Ganges River and watching "the burning Gahz." Steve remembered that evening. He didn't remember my poem. Just as well.

He was the same irascible, wonderful character thirty-six years ago when it came to poetry as he was right to the end. A few months before he died, the *Paterson Literary Review* published his op-ed-in-a-poem about modern poetry, "The Poets Are at It Again." Look it up. A kind of final bugle call from Steve.

I was emailing back and forth with Dorianne Laux about Steve (he was her first poetry teacher and close friend) and asked her who was going to wave the flag of clear and accessible poetry now that Steve was gone. She answered, "We all have to."

He was supportive to all poets no matter how they wrote. But if you were one of his close friends, he could be very, very direct. I took his last poetry class at Southwestern College before he retired. The class was filled with amazing writers all wanting to get one more "Steve fix." I had known Steve and exchanged poems with him for years but never took a class from him. I met many writers in that class, many who have become close friends. Steve was showing us poems that while we didn't exactly understand what the poet said, we knew what he meant. He used one line from Bob Dylan's "It's All Over Now, Baby Blue," the line that says "an orphan with a gun," as an example. Steve said we don't really understand this but we know what he means. Then Steve, waving his arms, sent us off for the night with the direction to go home and write a poem that had lines like that. I brought mine in the next week, showed it to Steve—he's standing at the front of the class, waves the poem at me and yells, "What is this Shit?" He had forgotten he gave us the assignment. All the "professional Steve students" had not written such a poem; they knew better. He was notorious for forgetting what he had assigned.

We would often walk along the beach in Pacific Beach and talk. It was on one of those walks when I told him I wanted to go back to college and get my MFA in Poetry. And what did he think of the idea. He asked if I thought I'd learn how to write poetry at one of those programs. No, I answered, I thought it was too late for that. If I wasn't doing it now, I never would. But I wanted an MFA so I could spend my last few decades teaching young poets in a college MFA program somewhere. Steve, as only Steve could be, wrapped his arm around me and said, "Forget it. No one's gonna hire an old shit like you." Ah Steve. No one talked to you straight like he did.

At readings, open mics, Steve was the first to applaud, the loudest, the last to stop clapping, always a big smile. He'd sit in the front row, had to, he couldn't hear very well. What you don't know is that often, he'd leave his hearing aids home. On those walks along Pacific Beach, the subject of open readings, open mics, frequently came up. Steve likened most of them to the experience of a root canal.

So, Steve, this is my gift to you tonight. This is an open reading. I am a poet. I am not going to read a poem.

Al Zolynas

A Philosophy of Life

To Steve Kowit

At the dinner party, Contessa, our hostess,
a lovely woman, though with a reputation
for not putting up with anyone's guff, bluntly
asked our friend Steve to cut to the chase and confess
his "philosophy of life"—mind you, right then
and there among the mushroom paté and roasted artichoke hearts—
that she didn't have time for niceties or beating around the bush, life was
too short, etc., all this after one of Steve's characteristically
misanthropic comments on human beings—he likes
to refer to us as *homo satanicus,* what with our long
history of wars, slavery, cruelty.
To his great credit, Steve took the question seriously,
paused, drew a deep breath, and simply declared himself
a skeptical mystic
or maybe it was a mystical skeptic.

Oddly, or not, this seemed to satisfy our hostess,
Steve not having much of a chance to elaborate beyond
referring to those moments we've all had
when everything pauses, or comes together, when all
is seen as connected, non-dual, miraculous, luminous—
whatever your favorite way of putting it.

At that moment, I deeply admired my friend Steve.
Indeed, what other "philosophy of life" could possibly hold up
in this paradoxical and heart-breaking world, this world
of leukemia and lollipops, catnip and catastrophe,
Abu Ghraib and avocados? The skeptic says, "I can't fully believe
anything you tell me because, really, how

the bloody hell do you know?"
And the mystic says, "Yes, like Rumi's, Dogen's, Teresa's,
and a host of others', my own experience is all
I can finally rely on, even though
I might be completely mistaken."

So, when the sun rises over the mountain
and the valley awakens with the mocking
bird's call and the coyote's (or wolf's, or dingo's, or hyena's)
last perplexed yip at the vanishing moon,
or when the walls collapse and we fall into
the bottomless black hole of
Stillness and Silence, what else, returning,
is there to say but yes, and yes again.
But, please, don't take my word for it.

[From Buddhist Scripture, Paraphrased]

Three things cannot be long hidden:
the sun, the moon, and the truth.

Third Portfolio:
A Selection of Kowit's Best-Loved Poems

[From *Steve Kowit Greatest Hits 1978–2003*]

I agree with Dylan Thomas that poetry is "inevitable narrative." I also love clarity, insight, and compassion. Like all poets, I cherish *le mot juste* and the perfect combination of sounds, and the phrase that is right enough to come with an almost audible click. . . .

A Prayer

If it weren't for Mary, who knows all too well my oblivious nature,
I'd never have noticed those tiny, crepuscular creatures
floating around in the dogs' water bowls. The big yellow
jackets are easy enough to spot & easy to save—you just
cup your hand under their bellies, tossing them free with a splash,
& they'll stumble back to their feet like indignant drunks, shake
out their wings, & fly off. But I'd never noticed those minuscule
midges & gnats till Mary pointed them out. At a casual glance
they are nothing but dust motes & flecks of debris.
By the time I bend over to look, a few have already been
pulled under & are hopelessly gone. But the ones still floating,
the ones still barely alive but alive nonetheless, you can lift out
on the tip of your finger, then gingerly coax onto dry cardboard
or fencing or whatever is lying around—though for godsakes
be careful! A single slip can prove fatal. But if you're patient
& steady enough, you'll see wings delicate as the lash of a small
child's eye at last start to flutter. What has been saved,
though easy enough to disparage, is somebody's precious,
irreplaceable life. Given this planet's unending grief, let us
save whom we can. Eons after the last hominid skull has
crumbled back into the loam, may swarms of these all
but invisible creatures' descendants coast still, at dusk,
over these hills. May they find water & food in abundance.
May every breeze upon which they sail prove benign.

A Whitman Portrait

You know that portrait of him that caused such a ruckus?
The one where he's propped in a cane-back chair
striking a pose so grave & heroic
you'd swear at first glance it was Odin or Lear or—
ah, but at that very moment you'll notice,
as just about everyone finally does,
the butterfly perched on his right index finger.
& then you can see that Walt's sitting there
under that rakish sombrero & beard, grandly amused,
as much as to say: *How splendid it is to see you, my dear,*
& what a propitious moment to call. . . .
You can guess how his critics stewed over that one!
They'd fling up their arms in maniacal fury
& swear up & down that the thing was a fraud.
Why, it's nothing but papier-mâché, they would shriek.
A cardboard & wire photographer's prop!
Which slander, however absurd & transparent,
the populace simply assumed to be fact—
till just last September when high-resolution spectro-
analysis proved what any fool could have guessed:
she was just what she seemed, mortal & breathing,
a carbon-molecular creature like us: *Papilio*
aristodemus, now all but extinct;
the very swallowtail, golden-banded & blue-tipped,
that archeo-lepidopterists claim
could have been seen all over Camden that summer:
one of the millions scooting about thru the woods
& fields around Timber Creek Pond. Only, for whatever
odd reason, this one had taken a fancy to Walt.
When she wasn't flitting about in the fennel & parsley,
the neighbors would see her light on his wrist
or swing thru his beard, or perch on his shoulder
like some sort of angel, or sprite, or familiar.

How he did it we don't know exactly,
but as the photographer set up his camera
Walt sat himself down by the open window
& hummed a few bars of Donizetti's *La Favorita*,
at which simple tune that bright little beauty
flitted in from the garden as if she'd been called to.
If it's true there exist fake butterflies
cut out of paper & wire, my guess is
they belong to a later generation of poets.
In any case, this one was made of the same stuff
as we are—felt pleasure & pain in abundance:
lit first on the broad brim of his hat, next
at his knee, & at last on his finger. Was greeted by Walt
with a gruff, friendly laugh as one of his cronies—
at which precise instant the chap with the camera
(he could hardly believe his remarkable luck)
pulled down the lever that triggered the shutter—
preserving forever that singular flight
of felicitous whimsy—this portrait at once majestic
& tender & bathed in affection & grace & delight:
Walt Whitman & butterfly. Camden, New Jersey, 1883.

Abuelita

At the Paso Picacho Campground just after dusk, I walk past a big Mexican

family picnic: everyone chatting & laughing around a long plank table littered

with paper plates & plastic cups & half-empty bottles of Fanta.

Two little girls off to one side collecting the prettiest stones,

& a slew of bigger kids racing around playing tag, wrestling & giggling;

& farther away, in a world of her own, a white-haired grandma

in a long green skirt is dancing ecstatically by herself, barefoot under

the stars, dancing with that invisible someone, her wide hips rocking

to music from an old Chevrolet's staticky speakers, the driver's door swung

open—the Dixie Chicks: *If I could only hold you now. . . .* Is it stupid

to guess she is dancing again as they danced when he was alive & both

of them young, that husband of hers, gone now, what—twenty, thirty years?

I walk through the campground toward where my own car is parked

this early November evening, the Pleiades gleaming above us,
    Stonewall Peak

darkening to the northeast, & a sliver of moon through the pines.

The others, chatting & laughing, pay her no mind as she sways there,
    eyes shut,

barefoot, lost in that old dream: a girl in her twenties, dancing again here in

Cuyamaca Rancho State Park, in her long green beautiful skirt,

with that boy whom she loves still, that boy she is going to marry.

Joy to the Fishes

I hiked out to the end of Sunset Cliffs
& climbed the breakwater,
sneakers strung over my shoulder
& a small collection of zen
poems in my fist.
A minnow
that had sloshed out of someone's bait bucket,
& that I came within an inch of stepping on,
convulsed in agony.
Delighted to assist,
I tossed it back into its ocean:
swirling eddies sucked about the rocks,
white pythagorean sailboats
in the middle distance.
Kids raced the surf,
a Labrador brought down a Frisbee,
& the sun sank pendulously
over the Pacific shelf.
I shivered & descended,
slipping the unopened book
into my pocket
& walked south
along the southern California coastline—
all the hills of Ocean Beach
glowing
in the rouged light
of midwinter sunset.
Even now
it pleases me to think
that somewhere
in the western coastal waters off America
that minnow is still swimming.

Notice

This evening, the sturdy Levis
I wore every day for over a year
& which seemed to the end
in perfect condition,
suddenly tore.
How or why I don't know,
but there it was: a big rip at the crotch.
A month ago my friend Nick
walked off a racquetball court,
showered,
got into this street clothes,
& halfway home collapsed & died.
Take heed, you who read this,
& drop to your knees now & again
like the poet Christopher Smart,
& kiss the earth & be joyful,
& make much of your time,
& be kindly to everyone,
even to those who do not deserve it.
For although you may not believe
it will happen,
you too will one day be gone,
I, whose Levis ripped at the crotch
for no reason,
assure you that such is the case.
Pass it on.

Poem for My Parents

For Michael & Billie Kowit
on the occasion of their 50th wedding anniversary

One night, back home in Brooklyn
after 15 years,
I sat around with Mary & the folks
going thru the books of their old photos:
pictures of my dad in knickers
in his late teens looking rakish
in a t-shirt & sailor cap,
holding the center pole of a pup tent—
in his early 20s, hitchhiking
to Montreal & drinking from a flask
at the side of a road.
Next to that, a piece of birch bark
that he sent my mother
from that escapade—postmarked Maine,
Sep. 2   7a.m. 1926. My mother
with a tennis racket, '27,
& smiling from a swimming pool in '28.
They are sitting on the railing of a ship;
my father in a bowtie & knit sweater,
she beside him, a lovely girl of 16,
their arms & feet touching.
They're just kids. They look beautiful,
both of them, the picture's dated
July 4, 1923.
& there's my mother with the Guild Players
in Disraeli & there they are
at Camp Allegro
surrounded half a century ago by friends
who have remained beloved to this day.
& then they're on their honeymoon

skating on a frozen lake
out in the woods of Pennsylvania
in the faded sepia gold of old snapshots—
a series of them
skating on the ice, holding hands,
my father with a pipe by a pine tree,
my mother leaning on the pillar of the house
where they were honeymooning,
hands sunk in her pockets,
her face gleaming. In the last
of that series, Mickey, my father,
has his arms around her,
they stand on the frozen lake
the woods behind them,
in their black skates & leather jackets.
He holds her to him.
They are radiantly happy.
They have just been married; it is December, 1928.
The ancient, black paper edges
of the photo album
as I turn the pages crumble
like confetti
& fall like tears.
Beyond the joy & tenderness & passion
of these early snapshots,
that are dated in the upper corners,
but which time has partially erased,
& against the zeitgeist: all fashion,
the grief of history,
& the drift of the age,
I honor them for the steady burning of their devotion.
May all of us be blessed by love
as faithful & unswerving.
They have been married 50 years.

2

Dad, one day over 30 years ago
you rigged a small sail
to an old rowboat
& we set off across a lake
high in the Berkshires.
It was the end of summer,
a day in August bathed in stillness.
I was a small boy, you
a strong, quiet man in your 40s.
Now & then small waves
slapped the thick sides under the oarlocks.
Then a wind came up so fast & quietly
we hardly noticed it until it seized us;
the small boat tossed about
bobbing like a cork. I
grabbed the sides, you worked the sail loose
quickly & unleashed it
& we drifted, oarless, far out,
waving our arms & fruitlessly calling out
to the few oblivious
figures on the dock, the sun
glinting ominously off those high waves.
Had it come to that we might have swum
for the other shore. Summers before
you had taught me: one hand
lifting my belly the other pressing
my back—I would kick & kick
holding the rope with both hands
squinting my eyes from the splashing.
Quiet, gentle, efficient, infinitely patient,
I think you are more
healer than teacher.
In those childhood illnesses,
I would wait hours for your figure
to appear out of the shadows of the hallway;

you would enter the room & say "Hi, Butch,"
& sit quietly at the edge of the bed.
& it was the same quiet reassurance of your presence
beside me that summer day, bathed in light,
when we were tossed about on the waters together,
which turned what might have become a small boy's panic
into a kind of bliss
that we were stranded
together,
alone, drifting. . .

& 30 years later felt the same bliss
when we swam together in the warm waters
off the coast of Miami. Alone
with you again I had the same experience
of your gentleness,
your quiet grace & strength.
Dad, I think your tolerance
& patience for the world
has been my strength for 40 years.
Odd, how little we have ever spoken to each other
& how absolute the love that has bound us.
The distance of a continent means nothing.
We are still together,
though older,
a man & his small son
drifting thru a void
that is turbulent & calm by turns—
marvelous beyond words, ineffable
& exquisite: silent
in a world of absolute stillness
on a lake that is infinite.

3

Ma, you stand at the dining room table & unfold
a paper napkin & place it, a white, translucent shawl

over your dark hair. Then you light two candles.
It is Friday evening. Outside the light is fading
from the world over Brooklyn, over East 14th Street,
with the darkness of early winter. As the room surrenders
to that darkness your white hands circle the small flames
of the two candles: they thin & flicker
under your fingers. Then you close your eyes
& recite the *brocha*. I can barely hear you.
An elevated Brighton Local rumbles thru the darkness
over Kelley Park. The shadow of your body
sways almost imperceptibly against the stairs:
How red your cheeks are in the light
of those two candles. Then the sound of the train
disappears & I hear you sobbing—tears
run down your cheeks.
You cover your face with your hands (perhaps
because I am there at your side in the dark room),
but your grief cannot be contained.
Your body trembles.
The candles, that are for the sabbath,
& honor the creation, are also, like the *yertzite*
candle burning in the glass in the kitchen,
for the dead. For your mother, Bertha,
my grandmother, who has recently died.
& as your grieving shadow sways & sobs
the *brocha*, you have become again
that small girl dancing down Second Avenue
more than half a century ago.
You are in a yellow dress, with ruffles,
you are carrying something home, some fish
or fruit wrapped in newspaper, a page
from the *Daily Forvitz*, you are dancing
among the pushcarts of Delancey Street,
you are dancing thru the door of the settlement house
& under the impoverished tenement stairways
of the east side.
In this family portrait your father's image

is dissolving as you & your brothers & sisters
blossom into your own lives.
Now you are married, now the chaos
of the great depression, now Mickey graduates
from law school, you give birth to a daughter,
& a son. The pitiless war like an evil wind:
your brothers disappear
for 4 years. They write from the battlefields
of France. There are tormented, desperate phone calls
in Yiddish. The Jews of Europe are slaughtered.
The screen door of the apartment in Bensonhurst slams shut.
Roosevelt dies. We move in with your mother in the Bronx;
Rosemont catches fire; you buy the house
on 14th Street: Camp Tamarack & the Pines,
& the black Plymouth & college for the kids
& Carol's wedding. Your son
kisses you goodbye & flies off to California.
It flickers, all of it, on the wall by the stairs
with your weeping shadow twenty years ago.
As I watch you there, in silence, helpless,
not just my mother now, but a woman, swaying
over the sabbath candles in the most ancient grief,
how my heart embraces you,
though I say nothing. Not a word. How dark it is
& how quiet. We are alone. Dad is dozing in the dark
in the other room. Carol is upstairs with her homework;
the last gray light of the day seeps thru the curtain.
A loaf of challah catches the light. It stands on
a silver tray on a white cloth. The tissue paper shawl
on your dark hair shivers in the flame
& glows with its own light.
& then it is done.
Your hands withdraw from your face.
The *brocha* ends. & the sobbing.
& when you take off that shawl all the past
disappears into those two, small yellow flames.
I wake Dad up, & standing at the foot of the stairs

yell for Carol to come down to dinner
& now you are taking the roast out of the oven & dad
does his funny cakewalk into the dining room,
that mischievous grin on his face & you say,
"Mick, don't be such a wise-guy, please"
& I laugh, & Carol sets the table & I
grab a piece of challah & dad grabs a piece of challah too,
& ma, you tell us to hold our horses & you
complain about having to put the roast back three times
but your face is beaming—your complaint full of joy
& I squeal I have to have gravy, I can't eat
anything without gravy. Carol brings in the potatoes
& we're all talking at once, the mindless
yammer of delight about the feast you have prepared
for us so lovingly—with such devotion—
that you have always prepared for us—
& it's great, ma. . . .
It's absolutely delicious—all these years,
the feast you have made for us all. Ma, it's wonderful.
It's absolutely wonderful.

Refugees, Late Summer Night

Woke with a start, the dogs barking out by the fence,
yard flooded with light. Groped to the window.
Out on the road a dozen quick figures
hugging the shadows: bundles slung at their shoulders,
water jugs at their hips. You could hear,
under the rattle of wind, as they passed,
the crunch of sneakers on gravel. *Pollos.* Illegals
who'd managed to slip past the border patrol,
its Broncos & choppers endlessly circling
the canyons & hills between here and Tecate.
Out there, in the dark, they could have been
anyone: refugees from Rwanda, slaves pushing north.
Palestinians, Gypsies, Armenians, Jews. . . .
The lights of Tijuana, that yellow haze to the west,
could have been Melos, Cracow, Quang Ngai. . . .
I watched from the window till they were lost
in the shadows. Our motion light turned itself off.
The dogs gave a last, perfunctory bark
& loped back to the house; those dry, rocky hills
& the wild sage at the edge of the canyon
vanishing too. Then stared out at nothing.
No sound anymore but my own breath,
& the papery click of the wind in the leaves
of that parched eucalyptus: a rattle of bones;
chimes in a doorway; history riffling its pages.

Taedong River Bridge

In memory of Jerry Greenberg

Retreating, Walker's 8th Army torched whatever lay in its path,
battered Pyongyang with rockets & mortars till the whole
besieged city crumbled in flame. Blew up the granaries, too,
& the bridges & roads, so that those who didn't freeze to death
would be sure to die of starvation—vengeance against the Chinese
Red Army & the peasant armies of North Korea for pushing them
back to Inchon. The U.S. command shelling that city till nothing
remained but that one standing bridge: tangle of girders with hardly
a place to find footing & nothing to grasp as it swayed in the wind-
driven sleet over those waters—Taedong River Bridge, the only
way left, short of death, to cross out of Pyongyang. Ten
thousand terrified souls swarming over its splintered ribs.
On their backs, in their arms, whatever they owned or could carry.
Women cradled their infants. Men strapped what they could
to their shoulders. The crippled & dying & blind inching their way,
for to slip—& hundreds of those fleeing slipped—was to vanish
into the icy hell of that river. Then the ones who watched, horrified,
would clutch one another & wail in that other language of theirs
while they kept moving. What else could they do? For what
it was worth, those who fell through saved the lives of those
inching behind them, letting them know where not to step next.

                                   Jerry, you saved my life
in much the same way. Now & again, in my mind, that awful black limo
pulls up at the curb in front of our house back in Flatbush,
& Henrietta, your mother, steps out, gaunt as death in that black
cotton shawl, while I watch from an upstairs window. At which moment
my own beloved mother slips into the room, lays a hand on my arm,
& tells me quietly, lest I say the wrong thing when her dearest friend
steps through the door, what she had hoped never
to have to tell me at all: that you had been killed at the front.

I was twelve. Forty years later I remain stunned. Now & again,
something triggers it back & I drift out to Kelly Park
& watch you fast-break downcourt—that long, floating jump
from the corner. The swish of the net.

                        Jerry, I don't know you'd care,
but when my number came up for the next imperial blood bath,
I gave my draft board the finger—for us both. And for every last
terrified soul on both sides. I can't tell you how grieved I am still
that you're gone. Or thank you enough for the warning: your death
letting me know where I stand, who my real enemies are,
what the heavy money had in store for me too.
In a way, then, I owe you my life: more than anyone else, you
were the one who showed me where not to step next
—the one up ahead, in the bitter wind of the past, who fell through.

[From *The Gods of Rapture*]

The terrible cry he let out
when he heard of her death
shattered the mountain
& pierced his own life
& he fell unconscious.
Child,
even now
when the deer remember,
the grass falls out of their mouths.

after Kṣemendra

Obituaries

[From "Song"]

We too
flapped our wings,
sang our brief song,
& were gone.

—from Kowit's book of poems *The First Noble Truth*

Tampa Review and Tampa Press

In Memoriam: Steve Kowit
(Friday, April 3, 2015)

The editors and staff of *Tampa Review* and the University of Tampa Press mourn the loss of poet-editor-teacher Steve Kowit, 2006 winner of the Tampa Review Prize for Poetry for his collection *The First Noble Truth* and author of other books of poems, including *Lurid Confessions*, *The Dumbbell Nebula*, and *The Gods of Rapture*. He also wrote the influential creative writing workshop text *In the Palm of Your Hand: The Poet's Portable Workshop*.

Steve passed away in his sleep in the early hours of April 2, 2015, at his home in Potrero, California, on Coyote Holler Road, in the San Diego area, near the Mexican border. We were in the process of editing page proofs for his forthcoming collection, *Cherish: New and Selected Poems*, which will be published later this year by the University of Tampa Press. He is survived by his wife Mary, who will complete the editing of this final collection.

Tributes can be found on Steve's Facebook page. He was a strong and vibrant force for poetry and a friend who will be deeply missed.

Tony Perry

Steve Kowit dies at 76;
San Diego poet championed numerous causes
(Los Angeles Times, April 12, 2015)

To Steve Kowit, the biggest sins that could be committed by poetry were being dull, obscure, too laden with allusions that might woo the intellectuals but turn off the common man (and woman).

His poem "I Attend a Poetry Reading" is Kowit's sendup of much of modern poetry and modern poets: *"Polite applause had stiffened / to an icy silence: / no one clapped / or nodded / No one sighed."*

As a poet, essayist, teacher and self-described "all-around no good troublemaker," Kowit was never dull. In a dozen volumes of poetry, his enthusiasm burst off the page in language that was direct, accessible and devoid of the ambiguity favored by some literary critics.

His poetic models included Walt Whitman, Robinson Jeffers and Allen Ginsberg, and he admitted in an essay titled "The Mystique of the Difficult Poem," that try as he might, he could not fathom poems, such as those of Hart Crane and others, that were "filled with footnotable literary allusions and hopelessly gnarled syntax and untrackable metaphoric acrobatics."

Recently retired from Southwestern College in Chula Vista but still holding poetry workshops at Liberty Station in San Diego, Kowit died April 2 of cardiac arrest at his home in Potrero in a rural stretch of southern San Diego County near the border with Mexico. He was 76.

He died just days before his latest volume of poetry is set to be published by Tampa University Press.

A story in *The Times* once described Kowit as "a pro, bard of innumerable liberal causes, a teacher, elfin, self-mocking, editor of a sassy volume of a no-intellectuals-need-apply poetry called *The Maverick Poets*." Among his causes, in poetry and prose, were animal rights and the plight of immigrants.

Steve Mark Kowit was born June 30, 1938 in New York. He liked to say that he was "Jewish by birth, Buddhist by inclination." He served in the Army Reserves and attended Brooklyn College.

In New York, he was part of the Lower East Side poetry-reading scene in the early 1960s. Later, attracted by the intellectual freedom accentuated by the Beat poets, he moved to San Francisco's Haight Ashbury and received a master's degree from then-San Francisco State College.

He taught at San Diego State, San Diego City College, UC San Diego and the College of Southern Idaho, and was publisher of Gorilla Press and founder of the Animal Rights Coalition of California. Among his books was *In the Palm of Your Hand: A Poet's Portable Workshop: A Lively and Illuminating Guide for the Practicing Poet*. His poetry was read by Garrison Keillor on his national radio show.

Part of Kowit's reputation among poets and poetry lovers came from poetry readings.

"He was a terrific performer," said poet and artist Austin Straus. "He could have been an actor; when he was onstage he was mesmerizing. He used humor to talk about matters of life and death."

Mixing passion and satire, Kowit poked at the "idiotic grandiosity of the human ego"—like his poem "The Workout" about the fitness craze of Southern California:

> Not unlike the penitents of other sects,
> they are convinced that decades of decay
> can be undone, & that the more one genuflects

the less one rots—a doctrine
that has got the aged, the adipose & the misshapen
pedaling their stationary bikes
in such unholy fury. . .

Still, the openness of Southern California appealed to him, like his poem "Joy to the Fishes" [page 216],

I hiked out to the end of Sunset Cliffs
& climbed the breakwater,
sneakers strung over my shoulder
& a small collection of zen
poems in my fist.

In "Refugees, Late Summer Night" [page 225], he sees the universality of the immigrants moving past his property:

Out there, in the dark, they could have been
anyone: refugees from Rwanda, slaves pushing north.
Palestinians, Gypsies, Armenians, Jews. . . .
The lights of Tijuana, that yellow haze to the west,
could have been Melos, Cracow, Quang Ngai. . . .

And in "Notice" [page 217], he wrote about the shortness of life and the death of a friend:

Take heed, you who read this,
& drop to your knees now & again
like the poet Christopher Smart
& kiss the earth & be joyful
& make much of your time
& be kindly to everyone,
even those who do not deserve it.

In "Crossing the River" [page 70], he brooded about life without his wife Mary:

In the bedroom, Mary has fallen asleep.
I stand in the doorway & watch her breathing
& wonder what it will be like
when one of us dies.

Kowit is survived by his wife, and his sister, Carol Adler.

A poetry reading in his honor is set for April 26 at Liberty Station, sponsored by San Diego Writers Ink.

Jewish Voice for Peace, San Diego [JVPSD]

Brilliant Poet, Ardent Activist, and Founding JVPSD Member Steve Kowit Dies at 76

Steve Kowit passed away in his sleep April 2nd. JVPSD has lost a deeply committed activist. We remember him for his enthusiasm, moral principles, gentleness, and intelligence.

A lifetime poet and teacher, Steve was never shy about challenging orthodoxies. At an early JVPSD meeting, he suggested dropping the word "Jewish" from the name of the group to emphasize a universal vision of humanity (he graciously accepted the rejection of his proposal). He was a whirlwind at demonstrations, animated, and sublimely happy! More than anyone, Steve kept alive the idea of a billboard campaign for San Diego after it had been officially put on hold, a campaign which recently came to fruition with great success. Thank you, Steve.

Steve was at his very best before a live audience, as a teacher and a poet, especially in reciting his own poetry. If the poet uses his own skin for "wallpaper," as one poet complained, Steve's skin was most sensitive to injustice. His poetry raged against the crimes of many, sparing no one. Some of his most moving lines decried the many abuses and indignities suffered by the Palestinians at the hands of Israel, supposedly in the name of the Jewish people.

Recently Steve read one of his searing tracts, the poem "Intifada," before a live audience at a local radio broadcast. Here, Steve was the angry poet in suspenders evoking empathy for the Palestinians and outrage at the depredations inflicted upon them. He didn't just "read" his poem; rather, Steve worked his audience by dramatizing his words, moving around, gesturing, and staring into faces. The result was unforgettable. This reading reflected his accessible, conscience-driven approach to poetry, a style which draws on the San Francisco beat poets of the 1940's and 1950's he admired in his youth.

Steve would also harness his pen for more prosaic tasks including a recent Op Ed in [*The San Diego*] *Union Tribune* [Is the U.S.-Israel love affair on the rocks?] that alerted San Diegans to JVP's billboard campaign against Israeli oppression and decried Israel's legacy of ethnic cleansing. He also published several well regarded essays on poetry.

In a recent email, Steve's widow Mary referred to her late husband's "wonderfulness." Steve did touch the lives of many, including his students as indicated by the many tributes his passing has prompted. We JVPSD members are most grateful for having Steve in our community and for providing us with moral sustenance and inspiration as needed. We all remember his persistent exhortation to speak the truth when it came to Israeli injustices. Steve will be sorely missed but his impassioned model for justice will endure in our hearts.

[From "Passing Thru"]

Do no intentional harm.
Even the least of these creatures,
the tiniest sentient speck,
longs to live out
its one brief season on Earth. . .

—from *The First Noble Truth*, by Steve Kowit

Kowit's Final Poetry Picks
for *Serving House Journal*

Assisted by SHJ editors
Duff Brenna and Clare MacQueen

Nearly five years ago, Steve Kowit began serving as Poetry Editor for *Serving House Journal*, with Issue Two. Issue 12 was scheduled to launch on the first of May 2015, but his illness and untimely death occurred before he could complete his review of all submissions for that issue.

Before he passed away, however, Steve had picked six "deliciously & outrageously erotic poems" by Alexis Rhone Fancher to publish, along with her brief commentaries on the poems.

He also chose an award-winning poem by Jeff Walt, "In the Bathroom Mirror this Morning," which Steve called "horrifying. . .in the best sense!"

The other poems in this section were chosen by SHJ Editors Duff Brenna and Clare MacQueen from among numerous works submitted during the reading period for Issue Twelve. (Poems which were contributed as tributes to Steve appear in this book under the "Tributes" section, beginning on page 159.)

Alexis Rhone Fancher

College Roommates

I asked for it, coming
home 2am, disheveled,
reeking sex. Every
weekend for a year.

It was my fault,
always in his face,
those skimpy clothes,
teasing him with
my inaccessibility.
I knew he knew I was
giving it away.

I wasn't surprised when
he sat in wait, pushed me
up against the dresser,
grabbed my breasts,
tore at my blouse,
ripped my skirt, shoved
himself into me, even
then, only half-hard.

I didn't mind the rape.
It was the softness I minded,
how he couldn't get it up
when it mattered.
I fell for hard men
with bad intentions.
Not men who loved me.

We never spoke of it

but his shame hung in the air,
that hangdog apology
in his eyes, the
unrequited love that
spoiled him for
anyone else.

Alexis Rhone Fancher

Handy

I wanted you small and folded
in my pocket. Like a Swiss Army knife.
Like a blow up doll. I wanted you
to fuck me and then disappear.

You wanted me wide open,
surrendered. Like a vacation.
Like a ripe nectarine.

I wanted to use you for sex.
Isn't that what all
men dream of?

You wanted to fuse us to the
bed, glue me, on my hands
and knees, to the sheet, through
the mattress, tether me to the box
springs, nail me through
the floor.

That day I saw you in Venice,
you walked past me
like your cock had
never been in my mouth.

I almost grabbed a fistful of you,
crammed you in like food.

Alexis Rhone Fancher

Dos Gardenias

I need to tell you how days drag now
that you're gone; no phone calls or Skype.

The light is never bright or warm. No one
wants to dance. Today I emptied an old bottle

of your pills, packed it with Hindu Kush,
drove to the beach. Lit up.

It's legal now in California.

I play your favorite music; Buena Vista
Social Club, Ibrahim Ferrer.

Remember that yellow bikini you used to wear?
It made you look invincible, like a star.

I'd wear the Che Guevara cap you brought
from Cuba when we danced, girl on girl
to *Dos Gardenias.* Our song.

Your breasts crushing mine.
Those signature gardenias pinned in your hair.

Now I dance alone, my screen dark.
I will not weep. You'd hate it.

Since you died, I play *Dos Gardenias*
every day, and the way the palm trees sway
breaks my heart.

You're out there, dancing,
aren't you?

Your yellow bikini a beacon, if only I could find it
in the star-crossed night.

—*for Kate O'Donnell*

Alexis Rhone Fancher

How I Lost My Virginity to Michael Cohen

1. My father hated him.
2. So his best friend, J.R., picked me up. Shook my daddy's hand at the door. Promised me back by midnight.
3. Daddy thought I was obedient, a good girl.
4. It was hot, even for August.
5. J.R.'s parents were in Vegas, so he loaned us their bedroom.
5a) They had a king-sized bed.
6. Diana Ross and the Supremes were singing Baby Love.
7. J.R. watched cartoons in the den.
8. Michael's middle finger furrowed between my thighs.
9. I felt that familiar wetness.
10. Except it wasn't my finger.
11. I remembered where I was and closed my eyes.
12. He pulled down my panties.
13. Pushed up my skirt.
14. No one had put their lips down there before.
15. No one.
16. It felt delicious.
17. I hoped he liked my scent.
18. There were lilies on the nightstand.
19. "Your hair smells so good," he mumbled.
20. He was holding his cock while he licked me.
21. I had never come before.
21a) Not like that.
22. It was then I knew I loved him.
23. He tasted like me.
24. His dick grew too big for my mouth.
25. When he entered me, it didn't hurt.
26. "I thought you were a virgin," he said.
27. I thought of the dildo that pleasured me in secret.
28. "Horseback riding," I said.
29. When the rubber broke, he promised he wouldn't come inside me.
30. He promised.

Alexis Rhone Fancher

The Narcissist's Confession

Before I was your wife I
was a narcissist.
Before that I was a dyke.

Before you I loved an artist. Big
cock. No ambition. I wanted him
to change. His cock shrank.

I poured sugar in his gas tank
to teach him a lesson.

What civilized person
acts like that?

Before I was your wife I loved a
woman. After sex
her scent lingered
on my upper lip.
Eau de Desperation.

But you, baby,
smell like success, old
east-coast money,
Episcopalian bebop, those
blue eyes focused Godward when
you come.

It took me forever,
stepping on them to get to
you. Sometimes
I wonder how

I managed to climb
over all those
bodies.

Alexis Rhone Fancher

White Flag

On Edward Hopper's painting Morning Sun, 1952

No one paints loneliness like he does. Those half-clad women by the bed, on the floor, hunched over, staring out the window, in profile or from behind, always clean lines, such worshipful light. The gas station in the middle of nowhere, estranged couples on the bright-lit porch after dark. Even the boats sail alone. And the diners. The hatted strangers, coming on to a redhead, a moody blonde, all of them losers, all of them desperate for a second chance. This morning the sunlight pried open my eyes, flooded our bedroom walls. I sat alone, in profile on our bed in a pink chemise, knees drawn up, arms crossed over my calves, staring out the window. Desperate for you. No one paints loneliness like Edward Hopper paints me, missing you, apologies on my lips. Come back. Stand below my window. Watch me beg for a second chance. Downturned mouth, teary eyes, parted knees, open thighs, that famous shaft of Hopper light a white flag, if only you could see.

Alexis Rhone Fancher

Commentary on Six Poems

COLLEGE ROOMMATES: I knew my shy, philosophy major roommate had a crush on me, and I'm sure I used him in that thoughtless way young, pretty girls do. When I drag-assed home that night, the last thing I expected to see was D., naked and determined. I didn't fight him. In my mixed-up head, I thought it was kind of exciting, until he couldn't perform. I wasn't cruel. I just took a shower and went to bed.

HANDY: The man in this poem stepped over the line. I wanted great sex. He wanted love. But I'd loved bad boys like him before, and it had always ended…badly. The sex *was* great, but when he told me he loved me, I made myself walk away. After it ended, I saw him one day on the Venice Beach boardwalk. He didn't see me.

DOS GARDENIAS was written for my bestie, the painter Kate O'Donnell, who died in 2014. What comes up after a loved one dies? How can you hang on to what remains? It was the first poem I wrote for her that I felt was any good. Her husband read it at her memorial.

HOW I LOST MY VIRGINITY TO MICHAEL COHEN is the title poem of my latest collection (Sybaritic Press, 2014). That night is so vivid it could have been yesterday. I was almost seventeen. We'd been dancing around my virginity for months. (His, too, although I didn't know it.) We didn't want to do it in the backseat of his car, so we made a plan. When I wrote the poem, it seemed natural to write it as a list.

THE NARCISSIST'S CONFESSION: This is one of those poems that shocks people, both at readings and on the page. I mean what's so shocking about a woman being brutally honest about her past with her husband?

WHITE FLAG: I'm a huge fan of Edward Hopper. His paintings, with their splendid sense of isolation, have room for whole stories inside of them. I was studying his painting *Morning Sun, 1952,* when the first line came to me. Suddenly, I *was* the woman in the painting.

Jeff Walt

In the Bathroom Mirror this Morning

new grey hairs in my beard numerous
as scattered headstones, scrutinize my crow's-feet.
Horrified of the day an orderly will lead me

by a fragile arm down a long, white corridor
in a nursing home called Eden or Camelot or Rainbow House
where even the flies are sick and fall dead

in mid-air and plants, desperate for water, hunch
dry and brittle, attendants forget the red emergency
light at their desk, kick back reading *People* magazine

as I choke on prunes, frantically
press the call button for help. I know I can't go back. Of course,
I'll never be sixteen again, kissing

Robbie Patterson on his single bed, rubbing his erection
through loose sweats, his mom watching *Guiding Light*
in the next room. Never again the years

I stayed awake all night, red-eyed, drunk, stoned, or both,
slumped over cold coffee in a ripped diner booth
with a man I'd just met on a dance floor

at Stallions, a sudden love that wouldn't last a week—years fallen
away easily as my hair that clogs this sink. Right now, I want
boyhood, Robbie again, wherever he is, our stupid plans

for happiness, saving coins to run away. All those years
back, not spider veins crawling up my legs, hairs coarse
as fir tree needles growing from my ears, applying

moisturizer and sunscreen and eye gel on my red, middle-age face,
ready for my slow commute through morning fog and darkness
in a dead man's used suit, tailored, perfectly fit. DJ on the radio

warns an icy storm to batter the coast: blames global warming,
flips on an old pop song so thrilling I remember Moon Dancing—
a world not doomed. Then how I forgot to fill my tank. Not certain

I've got enough gas to carry me, to forsake the worried world
and love it, and back into another irresistibly damned dawn.

Steve Kowit's response to "In the Bathroom Mirror this Morning":

Jeff, why do you have a hard time looking at your poem? It seems
pretty strong to me. Scary & dead ahead & of course has the ring of
truth. A horrifying poem. . .in the best sense! Can I reuse it in SHJ?
We'll mention in the bio that it won the Red Hen Prize? I'd be
delighted to use it.

Hugs, Steve

Jude Deason

Acorn

It began with an audacious
October. The sky blazed
and three apple trees blew red
like a warning
over the pasture fence

By November, the brick walk
was littered with the clatter
of oak, sycamore, ash
and behind the old barn,
the garden darkened
with the allure of gray weeds
and shiftlessness.

It is white now and winter.
The black dog buries her bone
and cold gathers in the farm house,
the hasp rattles, ruminates.

In the kitchen, I sit by the wood fire
with my dead father.
He polishes his shoes—
the ones he bought
when I was a child, five
pairs, half price, genuine
leather.

He's lined them up
like winter acorns.

Jude Deason

And We All Go Down Together

On the five-hundred-acre ranch,
my husband wears his cowboy hat
as he walks our dog to the barn
under smothering blue, high blue,
radiant blue, boundless   blue.

On television, thirty thousand fans
in Wrigley Field, Harry Carey,
the seventh inning stretch,
the sun-stroked shirtless bleacher bums
beyond the green diamond.

Our Chicago car is parked
not far from Wrigley Field
in the lot of the Catholic Abbey.
We early exit. We fast walk to beat the crowd.
"Too many people," I say. "Too many."

We have to cross the Rio Puerco in our pickup
to get to the hard road, fifteen minutes,
and fifteen minutes more to the women's restroom
that boasts that poster of Georgia O'Keefe
on the back of somebody,
on the back of a Harley,
her head cranked in reverse

with a face of happy in the desert, of in love
with this edgeless maze of empty
and the dead that grow needles, spindles, spikes, rocks,
the local enchilada.

Red chile, Green chile.
It doesn't matter.

My belly burns.
My city roots combust.
My smile is a mouthful
of rocks.

Jude Deason

In New Mexico, Another Lover

Before I go, I want to be a Joni Mitchell song.
I want to knock you back on the bed,
your awe staring at the ceiling,
your breath almost gone.

I want to lasso you in barbed wire
or capture you in a silken net and tack you
like a butterfly to a velvet board.
I want to lay open your wings.

You will love all things gorgeous
and tragic and flawed.
You will know you are not alone.
I will know I am a poet.

Michael Estabrook

Time Travel

Where has all
the time gone in his life
one moment
he's walking his girl
to her math class
next he's doing the after-dinner dishes
so her new nail polish
won't get spoiled
one moment
all he can think about
is kissing her
next he's waiting two hours
in the Orthodontics office
while she gets a root canal
one moment
he's obsessing if she'll really spend
her life with him
next he's reliving their first date
first kiss, their first "I love you"
over and over
and over again in his mind.

Michael Estabrook

Susan

She never said a word
not one word
to me in high school

but I never expected
her to why would she have she
was stunning—beautiful and confident

athletic and popular
with her blonde hair and tight
unstoppable teenage body

so when I received a Facebook "Friend Request"
from her I hit the "Accept" button so fast
I almost fell off my chair!

And yet I still had the audacity
to expect her to respond
to the dopey note I sent her:

"I just had to say hi
now that we are 'friends' on FB,
how are you?"

Of course she never responded
how could she, no of course she couldn't
reminding me that even after 50 years

some things never change
without upsetting life's delicate balance
reminding me that I should have remained

tongue-tied and awestruck, content
with my humble place
within the universe's unimpeachable physics
and oddly I am.

Tamara Hollins

The wind shifted, and 19 friends died

after the wind shifted
how many attempts were
there to reach you
how many phones rang
desperate hope
into the storm of the heat
how many loved ones placed calls
to phones that rang and then melted
as the saving color yellow dissolved into red?

Tamara Hollins

Absence

what was it like in the woods that day
when you walked to the cabin
swinging a basket by your side
did light dapple the earthen path
the pattern shifting as the wind shifted the leaves
did you see cardinals dart away
from an odd rustle that you couldn't hear
and wouldn't hear
until it was too late
was someone expecting you
waiting well past sunset
expectation turning to hope and prayer
did you somehow veer off the path
clinging to that basket
leaving only your absence behind?

Sylvia Levinson

I Attend a Concert

Too old to backflip, somersault—
trademarks of his wild man days,
tonight, paunchy, jowly, grand old man
still grinds fat-toned guitar licks, prowls
the stage lip, his black hair streaming,
eyes hidden under the brim of his brown
cowboy hat. He enters the crowd
and plays it sexy to the women,
plays it with his tongue, behind his
back, across his ass, and the audience howls.

We're all on our feet and
the darkened auditorium vibrates,
with shouts of "tell it, man," "oh, yeah,"
whoops and groans amid the blistering
pyrotechnics of Guitar Shorty. Grinding
blues, Texas shuffle, New Orleans funk,
his electric Fender screams, cajoles, seduces.
For a moment I stop my clapping,
head-bobbing and hip-shaking,
sit down in my seat and smile,
remember, this was the music
that once made me want to
take my clothes off.
It still does.

Paul-Victor Winters

You & Me & the Waitress & the Rest of the World

The waitress says she is no longer Cuban. You were once married to a Cuban, but you see no need to mention it. You order the Farmer's Omelet and you will probably slide your home fries onto my plate without discussion. Kids in a back booth play a game with their uncle's glass eye. On the wall-mounted TV, pods of orcas circle TV crews on boats and will continue until after nightfall. Researchers will discuss their complicated, clumsy, mouthy emotions. I don't realize I've been given the wrong order until I've already started in, and the TV shows a mother orca and her calf. One interviewer smiles awkwardly at a marine biologist, who is crying. Gas prices have been dropping, though, and we've avoided most of this season's hurricanes. We order more coffee. Two snowmobilers enter the diner and stomp the outside off of their feet. I recognize one of them from high school, but memory need not act once its eyes have blinked awake. And we ought to tip the waitress, who is at the end of her shift, and whose bus will arrive at its stop shortly. And there is a wait, I imagine—a growing line waiting for us to finish, just finish, bring the rest home in a bag.

Paul-Victor Winters

The Taking of a City

Because one religion works to defeat another. Because it is not the nature of the State to allow others. Rubble. Something that was once a marketplace. Partial wall of a partition, roads that lead only to rock piles. Because one has bronze and the other has iron. A field of horse bones. A grand staircase attached to nothing. Dog carcasses in a mound, near the skeleton of a church, shards of stained glass scattered about the dry soil. Because one archduke insulted another. Because one Emir went syphilitic and land-hungry. A falconer's empty coop, empty carts missing wheels, old women living in abandoned goat stalls. Because it's what we do. Because it is the Lenten season. Soldiers marching the main road, some without shoes. Rat hoards. Because strength is weakness. And for the sake of posterity. And for the hell of it.

Paul-Victor Winters

Family Tree

Gertrude off a bridge. Mathilda on a train track. And all of her children, save one, dead by twenty. The last time I ate blackberries was in 1775, crisp taste of change in the air. Grandmother cooked squirrel meat in gravy and served it over thick noodles. My sisters, Rheinlanders, continue to run from the ghost of a drowned uncle. Amsterdam. Ipswich. Aunt Winnifred. Grandfather Eudes. The first time I ate blueberries was a century ago. I arrived in a large steamship from Fredrikstad. I came to research lineage and to fight as a mercenary. Epke at the gallows. Hendrik by the rope. It is true we have weak stomachs and defiant livers. Christians with sticky fingers. Welshmen with gluttonous appetites for sins of the flesh. Obsessive compulsion from the Swedes. Gout from the Frisians. I am following my lost uncles. Forgive me for leaving, satchel of stolen, bruised fruit, swung over my shoulder. I have heard there is a large, new world worth visiting.

Paul-Victor Winters

Bonneville

Once, there was a blue Bonneville parked outside. And pines. No eviction notice was sent. Next door, the TV repairman and his sad wife. Across the street, a widow with walls of fading pictures and misaligned wallpaper stripes. And evergreens out front. It was summer, then it was fall. It was loneliness, then it was hustle and bustle. Once, the Mr. Chips truck parked in the widow's driveway. The mailman worked slowly. Once, there were several owls nesting in the eaves of a storm-shuttered roof. One clothesline for three families. Grandkids on weekends making a mess of crumbling curb-ends. Air thick with obituary slumber. Time is a sore loser. Even memory is sepia-toned. Pale mailboxes with bent red metal flags. Birdbaths moldy with autumn's divorcee leaves. Downed wires. Once, Christmas decorations hung in windows until March. Now, the hollowed-out cul-de-sac sinks, resigned foundations going weak, septics backing up. Time. All the yellowed junk mail adrift in the breeze. The ground a carpet of crisp, orange needles. Squirrels in the backyard sheds. The drafty windows are widows, now, too. Air thick and duo-toned. It was fall, then it was winter.

Paul-Victor Winters

Nightly News

And here, a story about our war,
told with a reasonable care.
A Jiggedy Jig and a Bumbley Bumb.

TV viewers are captive tenants
to councils, parliaments, and senates.
Bippity Boo and Dippity Dum.

Suicide blasts and no-fly zones.
Bags of bodies and boxes of bones.
Glibbity Glee and Glibbity Goo.

Between commercial breaks, blood.
Woulds, and *coulds,* and a *should.*
Lickity Split and Speckley Moo.

There is no end to this, our wars.
A Muckity Muck and a Globbity Gore.

Jeffrey Zable

Idealistic High School Weekend

told my old man to stick it up his ass
drank a case of beer
popped a couple of hymens
blackened 14 eyes
drove my chevy off a cliff
set fire to my homework
when i finally got in at 4 a.m.
what a weekend it was!

Jeffrey Zable

Dissertation on the Guillotine

If one was sent to the guillotine it meant that one's brain,
which controls the body, would no longer be influenced
by biological needs and reach a higher consciousness
explored in depth by a contemporary psychologist
named Abraham Maslow, who identified this state
as Self-Actualization.
If everyone had been guillotined, the world today
would be a more humane and civilized place
in which to live, but as history bears witness,
opportunities of this magnitude were reserved
for the privileged, which leads to the conclusion:
It's not what you know. . .but who!

Al Zolynas

Under Ideal Conditions

say in the flattest part of North Dakota
on a starless moonless night
no breath of wind

a man could light a candle
then walk away
every now and then
he could turn and see
the candle burning

seventeen miles later
provided conditions remained ideal
he could still see the flame

somewhere between the seventeenth and eighteenth mile
he would lose the light

if he were walking backwards
he would know the exact moment
when he lost the flame

he could step forward and find it again
back and forth
dark to light light to dark

what's the place where the light disappears?
where the light reappears?
don't tell me about photons
and eyeballs
reflection and refraction

don't tell me about one hundred and eighty-six thousand
miles per second and the theory of relativity

all I know is that place
where the light appears and disappears
that's the place where we live

Commentary by Zolynas on "Under Ideal Conditions"

As a long-time practitioner of Zen, I've been trained to pay attention to "what is," what's "just so" in this moment—our perceptions, our emotional states, our thoughts, our resistance, the ceaseless change occurring around us. In so doing, over a very long period of time, we come closer to simply appreciating the mystery that we dwell in and that we are. As a poet, I want to "record" some of that appreciation in language that is alive, interesting, and accessible. Doesn't the best poetry point us in the direction of that mystery? And doesn't great poetry help us to actually experience it?

Contributor Bios

Deborah Allbritain's poems have appeared in a number of literary journals such as: *Serving House Journal, Autism Digest, Perigee: Publication for the Arts* (Winter 2010), *The Michigan Quarterly Review* (Volume 30), *The Antioch Review, The Taos Review, Cimarron Review, Main Street Rag,* and *The New York Quarterly.* Her work also appears in several anthologies, including: *Stand Up Poetry* (ed. Charles Harper Webb; University of Iowa, 2002); *The Unmade Bed: Sensual Writing on Married Love* (ed. Laura Chester; Harper Collins, 1992); *The Book of Birth Poetry: An Eloquent and Ebullient Celebration of the Miracle of Life* (ed. Charlotte Otten; Bantam, 1995); *In the Palm of Your Hand: The Poet's Portable Workshop* (Steve Kowit; Tilbury House Publishers, 2003); and *A Year in Ink* (San Diego Writers, Ink). Her chapbook *The Blazing Shapes of this World* was published in 2003 by Laterthanever Press (San Diego). She works as a speech pathologist in San Diego County.

Peter Bolland is a San-Diego based writer, speaker, singer-songwriter, poet, and philosophy professor.

Duff Brenna is the author of nine books, including *The Book of Mamie,* which won the AWP Award for Best Novel; *The Holy Book of the Beard,* named "an underground classic" by *The New York Times; Too Cool,* a *New York Times* Noteworthy Book; and *The Altar of the Body,* given the Editors Prize Favorite Book of the Year Award (*South Florida Sun-Sentinel*) and also a San Diego Writers Association Award for Best Novel 2002. He is the recipient of a National Endowment for the Arts award, *Milwaukee Magazine's* Best Short Story of the Year Award, and a Pushcart Prize Honorable Mention. His book *Minnesota Memoirs* was awarded Best Short Story Collection at the 2013 Next Generation Indie Awards in New York City. His memoir, *Murdering the Mom,* was a Finalist for Best Non-Fiction at the same Independent Publishers Awards. His work has been translated into six languages, and he is the Founding Editor of *Serving House Journal.*

Tim Calaway resides in San Diego. He brings his varied experiences to life in his poems and stories of lost loves, lost dreams, and lost fortunes. His poems have appeared in several anthologies.

On the afternoon **Brandon Cesmat** met Steve Kowit at the Napa Valley Writers Conference, they talked about differences & similarities between poems and stories. When Brandon mentioned he played guitar, Steve asked him to play behind him that night, a performance they repeated several times, including for the 10-Year Anniversary of The Sunset Poets in Oceanside, California. Brandon's books include two collections of poetry, *Driven into the Shade* (winner of a San Diego Book Award) and *Light in All Directions,* and a collection of short stories, *When Pigs Fall in Love.*

Rebecca Chamaa is a writer who advocates for the mentally ill and is working towards an MFA in poetry at Antioch University in Los Angeles. She attends two writers' groups, one for poetry and one for memoir. Her poetry and essays have been published in *Transition, Structo, A Year in Ink, Pearl, City Works, The Reader, San Diego Poetry Annual 2014,* and elsewhere. She is also the author of the mixed-genre collection *Pills, Poetry & Prose: Life with Schizophrenia* (BookLocker.com, April 2015), and lives in San Diego with her husband of 17 years. Together they published an anthology of poets: *Sundays at Liberty Station* (March 2015).

Walter Cummins is co-publisher of Serving House Books and a faculty member in Fairleigh Dickinson University's MFA in Creative Writing Program. His seventh short-story collection, *Telling Stories: Old & New,* was published in 2015; and his sixth collection, *Habitat: Stories of Bent Realism,* was published in 2013. Cummins has published more than 100 stories in such magazines as *Kansas Quarterly, Other Voices, Crosscurrents, Florida Review, South Carolina Review, Green Hills Literary Lantern, Virginia Quarterly Review, Bellevue Literary Review, Arabesques,* and *Confrontation,* and on the Internet. He also has published memoirs, essays, articles, and reviews.

Jude Deason was born in small-town Illinois. After years of taking trips on horseback, she took a more radical ride, leaving Chicago and her profession as a licensed clinical social worker for life on a remote ranch in northern New Mexico. It was then that poetry entered her life in earnest. In her living room, she has a large piano which she loves, but she doesn't play it anymore, not after discovering poetry. Her poems appear in *Cold Mountain Review* and *Willow Springs,* and she has a poem forthcoming in *Briar Cliff Review.* Deason now lives and writes in Santa Fe.

Anna DiMartino is a writer, artist, educator, and mother of two. She holds a BA in Studio Art from UC Santa Cruz, and is currently pursuing an MFA at Pacific University in Oregon. Anna also works as the Director of a small non-profit preschool in Mission Hills. Her writing has appeared in *The Cancer Poetry Project 2; A Year in Ink, Volume 6* (San Diego Writers, Ink); and *Serving House Journal.*

Michael Estabrook is a recently retired baby-boomer poet freed finally after working 40 years for "The Man" and sometimes "The Woman." No more useless meetings under florescent lights in stuffy windowless rooms. Now he's able to devote serious time to making better poems when he's not, of course, trying to satisfy his wife's legendary Honey-Do List.

Alexis Rhone Fancher is a poet and photographer based in L.A. whose work has been nominated for three Pushcart Prizes and a Best of the Net Award. She is the author of *How I Lost My Virginity to Michael Cohen and Other Heart Stab Poems* (Sybaritic Press, 2014), available on Amazon. Her works have been published in *Rattle, Slipstream, Chiron Review, Ragazine, Cactus Heart, The MacGuffin,* and *Fjords Review.* Her photos are published worldwide. A total stage junkie, she is infamous for her recent Lit Crawl performance at Romantix, a NoHo sex shop, as well as for her readings all over L.A. In her other life, Alexis is poetry editor of *Cultural Weekly.*

Clyde Fixmer was born in New Mexico and grew up in Oklahoma. After serving in the USAF as a medic, he earned his degree at Oklahoma University, then worked at a number of colleges before moving to California in 1979. He taught writing for twelve years at an officer-candidate prep school in San Diego, and also at San Diego State University until he retired in 1997. He lives in La Mesa with his wife Kathy and their greyhound.

William **(Bill)** Harry **Harding** is an ex-Navy combat pilot, a novelist and former book critic, and the publisher of the *San Diego Poetry Annual.*

Terry Hertzler has worked as a writer and editor for more than 30 years. In addition, he has taught writing at the university level as well as for the Southern California Writers' Conference. His poetry and short stories have appeared in a variety of publications, including *North American Review, The Iowa Review, The Writer, Margie, Nimrod,* and the *Los Angeles Times.* His work has also been produced on stage and for radio and television. His publications include *The Way of the Snake,* a book of poetry on the war in Vietnam; *Second Skin,* a collection of poetry and short fiction; and several chapbooks.

Tamara Hollins has earned the following degrees: a B.A. in Art, with distinction, from Hendrix College; an M.A. in Cultural Studies from Claremont Graduate University; an M.F.A. in Writing and Literature from Bennington College; and a Ph.D. in English from Claremont Graduate University. Her scholarly work, creative writing, and art have been published in journals, anthologies, and encyclopedias. Her research interest is the production and the construction of identity in American literature. She is an Associate Professor of English.

Jackleen Holton Hookway is a poet-teacher with California Poets in the Schools. Her poems have been published in the anthology *The Giant Book of Poetry,* and have appeared or are forthcoming in several journals including *Bayou, Kestrel, Natural Bridge, North American Review, Permafrost, Rattle,* and *Sanskrit.* She recently won *Bellingham Review's* 49th Parallel Poetry Award.

Thomas E. Kennedy is the author of more than 30 books, including novels, story and essay collections, literary criticism, translation, anthologies, and most recently the four novels of the *Copenhagen Quartet: In the Company of Angels* (2010), *Falling Sideways* (2011), *Kerrigan in Copenhagen, A Love Story* (2013), and *Beneath the Neon Egg* (2014). All four are from Bloomsbury Publishing worldwide. In 2013, Kennedy also published *Getting Lucky: New & Selected Stories, 1982-2012* from New American Press. His books have been highly praised in the *Washington Post, The New Yorker, The Guardian,* and other prominent newspapers and magazines; and his latest novel was a recent Editors' Choice in *The New York Times Book Review.* His stories, essays, and translations from the Danish appear regularly in such venues as *The New Yorker Blog, The Independent* in London, *Esquire Weekly, Boston Review, The Southern Review, Epoch, Ecotone, New Letters, Glimmer Train, Broad Street, Writer's Chronicle, The Literary Review, American Poetry Review, Serving House Journal, Poet Lore,* and many others. His work has won the O. Henry Prize, two Pushcart Prizes, and a National Magazine Award as well. Kennedy has also won two Eric Hoffer Awards for novels, multiple grants from the Danish Arts Council, and other prizes and distinctions. He teaches fiction and creative nonfiction in the low-residency MFA program of Fairleigh Dickinson University and lives in Copenhagen.

Poet and young-adult novelist **Ron Koertge** grew up in rural Olney, Illinois, and received a BA from the University of Illinois and an MA from the University of Arizona. Koertge's poetry is marked by irreverent yet compassionate humor and a range of personas and voices. His poems are published widely and also appear in anthologies such as Billy Collins' *Poetry 180* and Kirby & Hamby's *Seriously Funny*. His latest poetry books include *The Ogre's Wife* (Ala Notable Books for Adults, 2013) and a collection of free-verse retellings of 20 iconic fairy tales, *Lies, Knives, and Girls in Red Dresses* (Candlewick, 2012). Other poetry collections include *Fever* (Red Hen Press, 2006), *Making Love to Roget's Wife* (1997), and a collection of ghazals, *Indigo* (Red Hen Press, 2009). Koertge also writes fiction for teenagers, including several novels-in-verse: *The Brimstone Journals* (2004), *Stoner & Spaz* (2004), *Strays* (2007), *Shakespeare Bats Cleanup* (2006), and *Shakespeare Makes the Playoffs* (2012) All five novels were honored by the American Library Association, and two received PEN awards. His honors also include a fellowship from the National Endowment for the Arts and a grant from the California Arts Council, and inclusion of his poems in two volumes of *Best American Poetry* and in Ted Kooser's *American Life in Poetry*. Koertge lives in South Pasadena, California.

Mary Kowit was born in Idaho and grew up in Minneapolis as the eldest of four sisters. She majored in art and psychology in college. Having explored many art forms, she now primarily focuses on copper enameling. She also works freelance as a proofreader and copy editor.

Sylvia Levinson moved to California in 1962 and to San Diego County in 1974, which she hopes qualifies her as a "local." Her poetry life began when she worked in marketing at the Old Globe Theatre for several years. She is the author of a chapbook, *Spoon* (Finishing Line Press, 2013), and *Gateways: Poems of Nature, Meditation and Renewal* (Caernarvon Press, 2005). Her work has been published in several journals and anthologies including: *Blue Arc West, City Works, San Diego Writers Ink, Magee Park, The Christian Science Monitor, The Reader,* and *Serving House Journal.* She believes "retirement" is an active verb which propels her poetry, workshops, volunteer work at KSDS Jazz 88.3 FM, and attendance at many theater and jazz performances each year.

Clare MacQueen is Editor-in-Chief and Webmaster of *KYSO Flash,* and she has served as copy editor and webmaster for *Serving House Journal* since its inception five years ago. She recently joined Queen's Ferry Press as Assistant Editor, Domestic for the *Best Small Fictions* series of anthologies. Her short fiction and essays have appeared in *Firstdraft, Bricolage,* and *Serving House Journal,* as well as in the anthologies *Best New Writing 2007* and *Winter Tales II: Women on the Art of Aging.* She won an Eric Hoffer Best New Writing Editor's Choice Award for nonfiction and was nominated twice for a Pushcart Prize. She and her husband Gary Gibbons designed and built custom websites as a team for nine years, and share avid interests in sci-fi movies, flower gardens, and urban beekeeping.

Born in Brooklyn to Arabic-Jewish parents who emigrated from Syria and Iraq during the first Depression, **Jack Marshall** is the author of a prose memoir, *From Baghdad to Brooklyn* (Coffee House Press, 2005), and thirteen books of poetry, which have been given a Guggenheim Fellowship, the PEN Center Poetry Award, two Northern California Book Awards, and a finalist nomination from the National Book Critics Circle Award.

Bill Mohr is an associate professor in the Department of English at California State University, Long Beach. He has a Ph.D. in Literature from the University of California, San Diego, and has taught at CSU Long Beach since 2006. His collections of poetry include *Hidden Proofs* (1982); *Penetralia* (1984); *Bittersweet Kaleidscope* (2006); and a bilingual volume published in Mexico, *Pruebas Ocultas* (Bonobos Editores, 2015). A CD and cassette release of spoken word was produced by Harvey Robert Kubernik and released by New Alliance Records in 1993. Mohr's poems, prose poems, and creative prose have appeared in dozens of magazines in the past 40 years, including *5 AM, Antioch Review, Beyond Baroque, Blue Collar Review, Blue Mesa Review, Caliban* (On-line), *Miramar, ONTHEBUS, OR, Santa Monica Review, Skidrow Penthouse, Solo Nolo, Sonora Review, Spot, Upstreet, Wormwood Review,* and *ZYZZYVA.* His poems have also appeared in a dozen anthologies, including all three editions of Charles Harper Webb's *Stand Up Poetry* (1989, 1992, 2002) and Suzanne Lummis's *Grand Passion* and *Wide Awake.*

Journalist **Tony Perry** serves as *Los Angeles Times* San Diego bureau chief.

A Southern California native, **Lynda Riese** lives in San Diego with her husband of 30 years and her two rescue dogs. She began to write seriously twenty years ago and has poems published in *Calyx, Onthebus, Poet Lore,* and other small press literary magazines in print and on the net. She also enjoys writing prose, and has an almost-finished novel in stories gathering dust in her desk drawer. When she's not writing or endlessly taking photographs of her dogs, she works as an antique dealer specializing in vintage and Victorian jewelry.

Non-fiction editor at *Serving House Journal,* **R. A. Rycraft** has published stories, poems, essays, reviews, and interviews in a number of journals and anthologies, including *The Book of Worst Meals: 25 Authors Write about Terrible Culinary Experiences* (Serving House Books, 2010), *Runnin' Around: The Serving House Book of Infidelity* (Serving House Books, 2014), *Pif Magazine, VerbSap, Perigee, The MacGuffin, Calyx, Contemporary World Literature, Del Sol Review,* and *The Absinthe Literary Review.* Her collection of short stories, *You Know,* is a *Web del Sol* World Voices chapbook. Winner of the Eric Hoffer Best New Writing Editor's Choice Award for 2008, Finalist for the Poets & Writers East/West Competition for 2010, and a Special Mention for the 2010 Pushcart Prize, Rycraft is chair of the English department and Coordinator of the Visiting Writers Series at Mt. San Jacinto College in Menifee, California. She is also co-editor of the Serving House Books anthology *Winter Tales II: Women on the Art of Aging* (2012).

Ron Salisbury lives in San Diego where he continues to publish, write, and study in San Diego State University's Master of Fine Arts program, Creative Writing. His work has been published in *Eclipse, The Cape Reader, Serving House Journal, Alaska Quarterly Review, Spitball, Soundings East, The Briar Cliff Review, Hiram Poetry Review, A Year in Ink,* and others. Awards include Semi-Finalist for the Anthony Hecht Poetry Prize (2012), Finalist for the ABZ First Book Contest (2014), First Runner-up for the Brittingham and Pollak Prize in Poetry (2014), and winner of the 2015 Main Street Rag Poetry Book Award, which includes publication of *Miss Desert Inn* in November 2015.

Jeff Walt's poem "In the Bathroom Mirror Each Morning" won First Place in the 2014 Red Hen Press Poetry Prize and was published in the *Los Angeles Review* (2015). He was Finalist in the 2014 Paumanok Poetry Contest sponsored by The Visiting Writers Program at Farmingdale State University, and was also a Finalist in the 13th Annual Gival Press Oscar Wilde Award, 2014, for "Each Day I Rise & Rot a Little More."

Paul-Victor Winters is a writer and teacher living in Southern New Jersey. He works for The Geraldine Dodge Foundation's Poetry Program and for Murphy Writing of Stockton College. Other poems have appeared in journals such as *2Rivers Review, Crack the Spine,* and *Shot Glass Journal.*

Jeffrey Zable is a poet, teacher, and conga drummer who plays Afro-Cuban folkloric music for dance classes and Rumbas around the San Francisco Bay Area. He's published five chapbooks including *Zable's Fables* with an introduction by the late, great Beat poet Harold Norse. His work appears, or is forthcoming, in *Coe Review, Kentucky Review, Tule Review, Pound of Flash, Rasputin, Clackamas Literary Review, Indigo Rising, Chaos Poetry Review* (featured poet), *After the Pause, Snow Monkey, Ishaan Literary Review, Lullwater Review,* the *2015 Rhysling Award Anthology,* and many others.

Al Zolynas was born in Austria of Lithuanian parents in 1945. After growing up in Sydney, Australia, he lived in Salt Lake City, and in Marshall and St. Paul, Minnesota. He has a BA from the University of Illinois and an MA and PhD in literature and creative writing from the University of Utah. At various times, he has been a poetry editor, resident poet in the schools, Minnesota Out Loud Traveling Poet, volunteer for the Hunger Project, and Fulbright-Hays Fellow to India. Retired from teaching since 2010, he now has emeritus status from Alliant International University, San Diego. Work by Zolynas has been widely published in journals and anthologies; and his books include *The New Physics* (Wesleyan University Press, 1979); *Under Ideal Conditions* (Laterthanever Press, 1994; San Diego Book Award, Best Poetry, 1994); and *The Same Air* (Intercultural Studies Forum, 1997). With Fred Moramarco, he is co-editor of *Men of Our Time: An Anthology of Male Poetry in Contemporary America* (University of Georgia Press, May 1992) and *The Poetry of Men's Lives: An International Anthology* (University of Georgia Press, 2004), which won the San Diego Book Award for Best Poetry Anthology in 2005. His works have been translated into Lithuanian, Spanish, Ukrainian, and Polish, the last by Czeslaw Milosz. He recently completed translating (from Lithuanian) the memoir, *The Parallels of Dita: Surviving Nazism and Communism in Lithuania,* by Silvija Lomsargytė-Pukienė and is seeking a publisher for the book. Zolynas practices and teaches Zen meditation in Escondido, California where he lives with his wife and two cats.

Acknowledgements

Works by Steve Kowit are reprinted here with kind permission from Mary Kowit.

"202 East 7th" is reprinted from *The California Journal of Poetics* (December 2014).

Three poems are reprinted from *The Sun*:

A Prayer (Issue 423, March 2011)
Abuelita (Issue 471, March 2015)
Taedong River Bridge (Issue 390, June 2008)

Reprinted from *Lurid Confessions* (Serving House Books, 2010):

A Swell Idea
Credo
Crossing the River
Cutting Our Losses
Hate Mail
It Was Your Song

Joy to the Fishes
Kowit
Lurid Confessions
Mysteries
Out of McHenry
Poem for My Parents

The Poetry Reading Was a Disaster
Wanted—Sensuous Woman Who Can Handle 12 Inches of Man

Reprinted from *The Dumbbell Nebula* (The Roundhouse Press, 2000):

A Trick
A Whitman Portrait
Kiss
Metaphysics
Notice

Rufugees, Late Summer Night
Some Clouds
The Black Shoe
The Blue Dress
The Prodigal Son's Brother

Three poems are reprinted from *The First Noble Truth* (University of Tampa Press, 2007), with permissions from Mary Kowit and the publisher:

A Betrayal
Theology
Will Boland & I

Several lines are quoted from the following poems from *The First Noble Truth* with permissions from Mary Kowit and from the publisher:

Passing Thru
Snapshot
Song
The First Noble Truth

Four untitled poems are reprinted from *The Gods of Rapture: Poems in the erotic mood* (San Diego City Works Press, 2006), each listed here by first line:

If she denies it she is lying
Let the flame of my passion
The terrible cry he let out
What chord did she pluck in my soul

"A Note Concerning My Military Career" is reprinted from personal email from Steve Kowit (July 2014) to SHJ co-editors. An earlier, prose version appears in *Socialist Viewpoint* (Volume 13, Number 6) which in turn attributes previous publication of the piece in *The Sun* (October 2013).

"Israel No Beacon of Democracy, Diversity" appears in the *Independent Record* (Helena, Montana, 18 August 2013) and is reprinted from:

http://stevekowit.com/political-essays/

"Mystique of the Difficult Poem" previously appeared in *Poetry International* (Issue 3, 1999) and is reprinted from:

http://stevekowit.com/essays/the-mystique-of-the-difficult-poem/

"Pablo Neruda Would Like to 'Explain a Few Things' to you" is reprinted from the *Union Tribune San Diego* (23 September 2007).

"Radicals, Rabbis and Peacemakers: Conversations with Jewish Critics of Israel, edited by Seth Farber" is reprinted from *Logos: A Journal of Modern Society and Culture* (Issue 5.2, Spring/Summer 2006).

"Stolen Kisses" previously appeared in *The Literary Review* (Volume 44, Issue 1, Fall 2000) and is republished here with assistance from Walter Cummins (Fairleigh Dickinson University).

"The 97,000-Mile-a-Minute Poetry Machine" is from *Light Years: An Anthology on Sociocultural Happenings (Multimedia in the East Village, 1960-1966)*; edited by Carol Bergé; Spuyten Duyvil, Small Press Distribution, Berkeley (May 2010).

"The General's Son: Journal of an Israeli in Palestine, a memoir by Miko Peled" was previously published as "Journey of Awakening: Life experience leads general's son to a compassionate view on Israeli-Palestinian conflict" in the San Diego Union Tribune (10 June 2012); and is reprinted from:

http://stevekowitcom/political-essays/

Illustrations by Mary Kowit are reproduced here with her permission:

Frog:	Dedication page
Self-Portrait:	Page 73
Checkers:	Page 129
Penguins:	Page 243

"A Few Words about Steve Kowit," a review by Duff Brenna, was first published in *Serving House News* (3 November 2010) and appeared later in *KYSO Flash* online (Issue 1, Fall 2014).

"The Chiron Interview" of Steve Kowit by Terry Hertzler was first published in *Chiron Review* (summer 2004). It appears here with permission from the author and is reprinted from:

http://stevekowit.com/the-chiron-interview/

"Brilliant Poet, Ardent Activist, and Founding JVPSD Member Steve Kowit Dies at 76," is reprinted from the Jewish Voice for Peace, San Diego (JVPSD) website.

"Steve Kowit Dies at 76; San Diego Poet Championed Numerous Causes," an obituary by Tony Perry, is reprinted with the author's permission from the *Los Angeles Times*:

http://www.latimes.com/local/obituaries/la-me-steve-kowit-20150413-story.html

"In Memoriam: Steve Kowit" is reprinted from the *Tampa Review and Tampa Press* blog (3 April 2015).

"In the Bathroom Mirror this Morning" by Jeff Walt is reprinted from *The Los Angeles Review* (2015).

The following tributes are reprinted here from Issue 12 of *Serving House Journal*, with permissions from their respective authors:

Deborah Allbritain: "Sappho Learns of Your Death"

Peter Bolland: "[A Pillar of Our Own Reach]"

Duff Brenna: "Something about Steve"

Tim Calaway: "The Poetry Teacher"

Brandon Cesmat: "Dinners To-Go"

Rebecca Chamaa: "The Last Act" and "The Most Meaningful Memorial"

Jude Deason:
    Acorn
    And We All Go Down Together
    In New Mexico, Another Lover

Anna DiMartino: "A Cricket's Prayer"

Michael Estabrook: "Susan" and "Time Travel"

Alexis Rhone Fancher: Six Poems, plus Commentary:
    College Roommates
    Dos Gardenias
    Handy
    How I Lost My Virginity to Michael Cohen
    The Narcissist's Confession
    White Flag

Bill Harding: "[A Genuine Treasure]"

Tamara Hollins: "Absence" and "The wind shifted, and 19 friends died"

Jackleen Holton Hookway: "The Poetry Lesson," plus Commentary

Bill Mohr: "Steve Kowit (1938-2015)" and "Steve Kowit Postscript: Walt Whitman's Butterfly"

Sylvia Levinson: "I Attend a Concert" and "My Steve Kowit"

Lynda Riese: "His First Day in Heaven" and "Like Wings"

R. A. Rycraft: "Don't Laugh at My Poetry!"

Ron Salisbury: "[A Tribute]"

Paul-Victor Winters:
 Bonneville
 Family Tree
 Nightly News
 The Taking of a City (republished in SHJ-12 from *Full of Crow*, October 2013)
 You & Me & the Waitress & the Rest of the World

Jeffrey Zable: "Dissertation on the Guillotine" and "Idealistic High School Weekend"

Al Zolynas: "A Philosophy of Life" and "Under Ideal Conditions," plus Commentary

---

The following works are published here for the first time:

Clyde Fixmer: "Dear Mary"

Terry Hertzler: "The Golden Years"

Thomas E. Kennedy: "The Stand-Up Poet"

Ron Koertge: "[Bringing the House Down]"

Jack Marshall: "Steve Kowit"

List of Kowit Poems Reprinted in This Book

Some Clouds

Now that I've unplugged the phone,
no one can reach me—
At least for this one afternoon
they will have to get by without my advice
or opinion.
Now nobody else is going to call
& ask in a tentative voice
if I haven't yet heard that she's dead,
that woman I once loved—
nothing but ashes scattered over a city
that barely itself any longer exists.
Yes, thank you, I've heard.
It had been too lovely a morning.
That in itself should have warned me.
The sun lit up the tangerines
& the blazing poinsettias
like so many candles.
For one afternoon they will have to forgive me.
I am busy watching things happen again
that happened a long time ago,
as I lean back in Josephine's lawnchair
under a sky of incredible blue,
broken—if that is the word for it—
by a few billowing clouds,
all white & unspeakably lovely,
drifting out of one nothingness into another.

Goodbye, Farewell, Be Well.

Hugs, Steve